PRAISE FROM READERS

"This positivity, resilience and outlook Dwania had throughout her journey as told in this book truly was and is a great example for all of us to remember, and to continue to remindour selves in our day to day. Told with gratitude, humour, sadness and realism, I appreciated Dwania's honestly and courage in sharing her personal journey with us. This books is truly a must-have for all of us, as we all know people who have received a cancer this diagnosis; and wondered what to say, how to support and want to understand what they are going through. Thank you Dwania."

—Kristin Thomas
Director, Philanthropy
Trillium Health Partners Foundation

""Tomorrow is Another Day" is an extraordinary story of resilience. I loved the author's attitude of positivity and immense trust in the doctors and the medical system. I also loved how she deals with cancer no more than just one more thing in her life. The narrative unfolds with her doing cancer, visiting her hair dresser, travelling, doing Thanksgiving and birthdays

with the same spirit that someone without cancer would do. Her message from her story is that life is life-ing and she demonstrates what it looks like to be alive, to savour life, to live it with gratitude, to make every moment count, to enjoy every encounter and to be happy to be alive. Her sense of humour is very uplifting and shows us how to transform our fears around cancer treatment and give it a funny twist. I laughed when she asks the doctor if she is getting new boobs and admire her vulnerability. I was inspired when she saw her "buzz cut" moment as freeing or her medicine as "drug cocktails" for chemo. Her love for her family is so moving.

This is a story about the relentless spirit of a human who loves her life. From the very first page, she took me in. I cried with her and laughed with her, travelled vicariously with her and stayed with her throughout the book.

This book is the story of a Cancer Hero. The world needs this super dose of positivity and hope!"

—Shirin Ariff
Cancer Hero, 6x International Bestselling Author
Resiliency Coach and Award winning Speaker

"Dwania she wrote this book documenting her cancer experience from diagnosis to recovery to inspire and guide those going through cancer, especially women who are suffering breast cancer. I find this the perfect guide for partners, friends, and family who know someone that has been diagnosed.

As a scientist and a people planner, Dwania speaks of her experiences in a way that is accurate without being precise. By weaving in her travels to London, Portugal, and Jamaica, Dwania gives the reader an understanding of all the medical procedures without feeling like cancer is a sentence to bed and puking. She offers a view that is honest and hopeful without being overly saccharine.

Read. Learn. Understand. Journey.

This book is for people who are overly suspicious of people who say they are truly thankful for having suffered."

—Sasha-Li Chinloy
Chief Strategist & Executioner

"*Dwania's story, actually her love letter to life, takes you on a remarkable journey. She shares this challenging chapter of her inspiring life in the form of a conversation. You feel as if you were right there beside her every step of the way. Not only do you feel as if you are holding her up during this emotional roller coaster ride, there is a sense of pride with how she takes on this battle with such grace and strength. You may cry, you may scream "why", but you most definitely shout out the loudest cheers of encouragement for this Princess Warrior. This story is a must read because Dwania so eloquently shares parts of her cancer journey you don't normally hear about. She is fearless, honest and the forever optimist. I am thankful for this book and even more thankful for Dwania McLarty-Peele. We are blessed to say Tomorrow is Another Day.*"

—Roxane Henry

TOMORROW IS ANOTHER DAY

Dwania McLarty-Peele

Tomorrow Is Another Day
Dwania McLarty-Peele

ISBN: 978-1-956193-96-1
Book Design & Publishing done by:
Global Book Publishing
www.globalbookpublishing.com

I dedicate this book to all my superheroes in the medical field, especially those at the Bustamante Hospital for Children in Jamaica and Credit Valley Hospital in Ontario, Canada.

Table of Contents

Preface

As a child in Jamaica, life was simple. My job was to go to school and do well. I took pride in always being at the top of my class. I excelled at everything I did. That included having fun. My family can attest that I was always fun-loving. I liked to try new things. Some of my favorite memories were spent at the beach, at the zoo or running around the yard with my God-brother. Sitting under a fruit tree and soaking up the sun was one of my after-school pleasures.

A guilty pleasure of mine was spending time around my mother's adult friends and getting a peek at what my adult life could be. I dreamt that I would be a doctor or someone in the medical field, living in the hills of Jamaica and taking lavish vacations. I couldn't wait to experience making my own decisions and driving. I was obsessed with being able to drive.

When I was eleven, my life changed drastically. I left my sweet island in the sun and moved to New York City. There were layers of shock. I had to get accustomed to life in the cold, a blend of people from many backgrounds, different foods, different personalities, and a more liberal way of life. I found myself defending my culture and my level of intelligence on more occasions than I would like to discuss. I experienced my first of many bouts of racism. The lessons that I learned while living in NYC forced me to grow up quickly and to always be ready to fight for what I earned. For eight years, the concrete jungle of NYC was my home. All my experiences made a huge impact on who I am today.

Since then, I have moved to yet another country—Canada. My first experience in Toronto involved me volunteering at Toronto General Hospital. I wanted to find a way to immerse myself in one of my favorite places and spread some love to patients in need. The transition from the United States to Canada was much easier than my earlier move from Jamaica to the United States. Between the ages of eighteen and thirty-nine, I have done more things than I could have imagined. I worked in many industries, moved to a new city for school, started a career and two businesses.

A new city brought new dreams. I realized that my love of freedom and flexibility meant that a life in medicine was not for me. Instead, I wanted to be in science in some other form. After much thought and research, I decided I wanted to work in a lab setting. I received my Diploma in Chemical Laboratory Technology from St. Clair College of Applied Arts and Technology. I also earned two Bachelor's Degrees from the University of Windsor—one in Chemistry and the other in

Political Science. I was fortunate enough to start my career in Windsor while going to school. That experience gave me the confidence I needed to surge forward with other opportunities.

Windsor was also the place where I met my wonderful husband. After ten years, we decided to make a move together to the Toronto area. This move injected new and fun experiences into our lives. It gave me a chance to re-experience the city as a true adult. I didn't get caught up in the hustle of being an adult because enjoying my life was always a high priority. That love of living a full and exciting life did not stop when I was suddenly diagnosed with breast cancer.

So here we are. I start this story by taking you back to when I fell in love with my first super heroes. Follow my experience over the period of approximately one year, where I share my journey of slaying this dragon called cancer.

Resilience Checklist

- ☐ **Acknowledge Your Strengths:** Recognize your unique skills, talents, and experiences that have brought you to where you are today.

- ☐ **Define Your Goals:** Clearly define your short-term and long-term goals, breaking them down into manageable tasks to stay focused and motivated.

- ☐ **Seek Support:** Build a strong support network of mentors, peers, and professionals who can offer guidance, advice, and encouragement during challenging times.

- ☐ **Practice Self-Care:** Prioritize your physical, mental, and emotional well-being by incorporating self-care activities into your daily routine, such as exercise, meditation, or spending time with loved ones.

- ☐ **Adaptability:** Embrace change and be willing to adapt your strategies, plans, and approaches as needed to navigate unforeseen challenges and obstacles.

- ☐ **Learn from Setbacks:** View setbacks and failures as opportunities for growth and learning, extracting valuable lessons that will help you improve and succeed in the future.

- ☐ **Stay Positive:** Cultivate a positive mindset and focus on the opportunities and possibilities that lie ahead, even in the face of adversity.

- ☐ **Celebrate Progress:** Acknowledge and celebrate your achievements, no matter how small, to boost your confidence and motivation along the way.

- ☐ **Stay Resilient:** Stay resilient in the face of adversity, maintaining your determination and perseverance to overcome challenges and achieve your goals.

- ☐ **Reflect and Reassess:** Regularly reflect on your progress, reassess your goals and strategies, and make adjustments as necessary to stay on track and continue moving forward.

INTRODUCTION

Imagine yourself in a bubble. A bubble? Yes, *I* was the girl in a bubble. I still have vivid memories of lying on a white metal hospital bed with chipped paint. I was in the Bustamante Hospital for Children in Jamaica. Quite a few nurses surrounded me. I was hooked up to an IV and Ventalin®-infused oxygen was being fed into my little "bubble" so that I could breathe. I spent so much time in large rooms filled with beds like mine, with other asthmatic children like myself. I spent birthdays and many holidays in *that* bubble. It became my home away from home. I did homework in that bubble. I remember being able to leave feeling better each time I was admitted and stayed in that bubble. I remember the look on my mother's face when I was able to go home. The gratitude. The relief. I remember it all.

Looking back at moments like these reminds me of my love for medicine and medical professionals. When thinking of my superheroes, the only people who come to mind are medical professionals. After spending as much time in hospitals as I did, one would think that I would be terrified of the place and of doctors! Did you know there is a term for that? It's called *white coat syndrome* and is often experienced by people who have had intense medical experiences. For me, it is quite the opposite. I adore medical professionals. I love everything about hospitals. It's the perfect place to be when you are not your best. In my experience, they have always fixed me up and sent me on my way, so it's only natural that when diagnosed with breast cancer, I didn't have a worry in the world. I figured that my superheroes had this under control, and the pandemic hit. Imagine going through the motion of cancer treatment and just when you feel you are almost at the end of the treatment journey and the celebrations should begin, there is a once-in-a-lifetime pandemic. Panic did indeed set in. This was something that none of us could foresee, let alone know how to handle.

1

The Lump

A state of emergency. Words I don't expect to hear or necessarily want to hear while going through breast cancer treatment. The world is currently going through what is being dubbed a pandemic. This is a once-in-a-lifetime experience. This pandemic has been wreaking havoc on other parts of the world. Before today, this wasn't really at the forefront of my mind. COVID-19, as the virus is being called, is an anomaly to us all. So, imagine hearing that it is now in your backyard, and it is spreading like wildfire, to top it off, there is nothing the medical professionals or anyone can do about it.

As this state of emergency was being declared, I was sitting in my car with my nephew Darius, getting ready to drop him off at his summer program. I had 30 minutes to get him settled and make it to my radiation appointment at the hospital. I pulled up to his school and received a call from the Principal informing me that summer school was closing due to a state of emergency. With this announcement, everything had changed. Summer school was canceled. We were now faced with the unknown. In other countries, there were severe lockdowns. People were quarantined in their homes and not allowed to leave unless given special permission. Is that what we would be facing going forward? I had zero time to worry and a few hours to strategize. As we headed to the hospital, I was concerned about how this would change the state of how we operate. Would this change my treatment plan? Would I be able to complete my treatment?

As we arrived, we were presented with what seemed like the first hurdle. My nephew was only nine years old, and the oncology wing of the hospital did not allow children under the age of sixteen inside for safety reasons. Under the given circumstances, extra precautions were already taken upon entering the hospital. Speaking with security and senior hospital staff, they were kind enough to arrange for my nephew to wait at the reception and be supervised by administrative staff while I received my treatment. Day by day as I showed up for treatment with my nephew, I started to feel more panicked. This pandemic was something new for everyone. With the death rate being as high as it was in Italy, it was difficult to not think of the worst. Each day, I watched the news to see the numbers being released by health officials. How many new cases? How many deaths? How many tests were being performed? How many surgical procedures were being canceled? Would we get through this? Would I get through this?

My mind was racing a million miles per second. At this point, cancer treatment was not my greatest concern, but surviving this pandemic surely was. The unknown is frightening. Leaving the house daily—even for treatment—was becoming more and more terrifying with each day. As the days went by, my level of anxiety for my health, my family, and my friends, was heightened. This time, the feeling spanned over days. The last time I felt this anxious, minutes felt like days...

I had lumps in my breast for about three years prior to this diagnosis. My doctor has always been diligent in monitoring them by having me do annual ultrasounds. I have always been punctual with my appointments and have always taken his advice. I still recall him saying, "If ever you feel pain in the area where the lumps are, come and see me immediately." This statement has always been running over and over in my head, so when I started to think I felt pain in the area while doing my jumping jacks in boot camp or while running down the stairs, you can imagine my concern. I was a bit hesitant in acting on the pain as I wanted to be certain it wasn't only hurting during my menstrual cycle as breasts normally do or that it wasn't just in my head. After a few months of monitoring, I felt it was time to go in and have that conversation.

I recall sitting in that office and telling my general practitioner that the lump in my right breast had started to hurt continuously and that the pain was heightened whenever I was moving. I remember telling him I was certain and that the pain was not in my overall breast, but it was a deep pain that I felt in the lump. He immediately gave me a requisition for a breast ultrasound.

Having a breast ultrasound has been standard practice for me, so it felt like just another day in the office—but that was until I was changing back into my clothes and the technician requested me not to. That was the precise moment when I knew this was not just another ultrasound. I was in the change room going through all possible scenarios and preparing myself for the worst. Are the results inconclusive? Did they see something that is making them concerned? What happens next? Little did I know, this was going to be the start of a whole new journey in my life.

Continuing along with day-to-day tasks with something as heavy as the possibility of cancer on my mind was not easy. It was a constant exercise of positive thinking and manifestation. I had to find a balance between being realistic about what the outcome could be while hoping for the best possible scenario. There was and still is no guidebook to prepare for this.

I took that time as an opportunity to surround myself with positivity. I booked lunches and dinners with friends constantly in order to keep my mind focused on fun activities. In moments where I found myself drifting off into the abyss of negativity, I would find something entertaining to watch online. There were also times when I found myself sitting in my car in the park, people-watching. I began making up stories for the people I watched. Some were fun and exciting tales, while others had a level of sadness to reflect what could be my reality. I wondered how many of them were also making up stories about me. What was my story in their eyes? I hoped it had a happy ending.

2

The Mammogram

The world stood still. To be honest, I was yearning for things to get back to normal. My level of impatience was growing and all this silence was deafening. I had to admit that at first, it was a relief to know that everyone was being forced to stay home. It felt like a different world. It also felt like I was on an even playing field with everyone and that I wasn't missing out on any exciting social events.

Day by day, the level of uncertainty grew. There were no answers, just sickness and death. The news stations began tallying the growing number of COVID-19 cases as well as the number of reported deaths. The level of anxiety I felt each time I scrolled past a news channel was enough to pivot me to streaming services. This way, my mind could be in constant euphoria. There was no need to be interrupted by the reality of the world. It felt as if the earth was off its axis and was tumbling into the vastness of the universe with no end in sight.

This virus was now hitting too close to home. I began getting word of people close to me getting sick. There started to be a level of panic if anyone had a cough. Our hands were tied. We became accustomed to ordering all of our needs online. We were vigilant in sanitizing everything before it came into the house—even our mail. No one, under any circumstances, was allowed inside. It was indeed a lockdown.

While we waited, my husband and I tried to sift through the confusion to find all the positives. Putting things into perspective while we waited helped ease our minds. This lockdown gave us the chance to spend more time together and enjoy our home. For him, there was the joy of no commute and huge savings on fueling up the cars. I must admit, time was moving slowly. My patience was waning. I needed to get back to normal, or at least, a resemblance of normal. Every day started feeling the same, much like it did during my cancer treatment.

As I sat in that change room waiting for the technician to return, once again minutes felt like days. My mind was chattering away. While I waited in the change room, I kept thinking about all the other times I did an ultrasound. I was willing this moment to be just like the others. I also started preparing myself mentally to receive and accept whatever news was to come. I started to wonder how I would deliver the news to my loved ones, fearing if it was unpleasant. My mind was going in circles.

The technician returned and asked me if I had ever had a mammogram before. The answer was no. She then told me that based on the preliminary results of the ultrasound, it is advised that I should have a mammogram done right away.

Dear Reader, if you have never done a mammogram, I highly recommend that you book your appointment now! Allow me to enlighten you—not frighten you. The process involved standing in a variety of awkward positions, holding my breath, and having my breast squeezed tightly and almost flattened between two metal "plates." This is not the *Fifty Shades of Grey* that I fantasized about. I don't consider myself to have large breasts, but all I kept thinking during the process was how much more difficult it would be if I had smaller ones! As a newbie, I needed a lot of guidance. The technician eased me into the position and tried to make the process as easy as possible. After about 10 minutes of "breast acrobatics" I was finally done. I exhaled, thanked the technician, and as I walked back to the change room, I was in a daze. It was at that moment; I knew my life would never be the same again.

3

The Results

Lakefront cottage, barbecue, wine, buckets of Sangria and good girlfriends are what the official kickoff to summer looks like! Typically, we would be busy planning; making grocery lists, making alcohol lists, making menus, and planning car pools. Instead, we are deep in a pandemic, and what would normally be my first real getaway of the year is now canceled.

Over the past seven years, our group of girlfriends have blocked off this May long weekend on our calendars. We rent a cottage in different regions each time and vow that the weekend will be about relaxing, recharging, and reconnecting. For some of us ladies, this is the only time we see each other for the entire year. For most of us, it is time away from our families and a way to reset.

This year in particular was the year I was truly looking forward to. It would be the bookend to my saga. I found out about my diagnosis as I was getting ready for a vacation, so it would only be fair to finish treatment and go on a vacation—a mini vacation really. I imagine sitting on a deck and enjoying the fresh air and sunshine while catching up on each other's lives and chatting about our favorite TV shows—usually reality shows. Taking a day to check out what the small town had to offer and the tradition of finding an ice-cream joint and diving right in was on the agenda.

All my vacation dreams have come to an end with this pandemic. Who knows when the next trip will be. The world is in limbo.

I can admit that waiting is not my superpower. I am rather impatient. Trying to continue with the motions of my regular life while waiting for my life to change was confusing my psyche. I should have been joyously planning my long awaited European vacation and dreaming of sight-seeing, of the foods I would eat, and of the people I would meet. Instead, I was waiting.

Sitting in my doctor's office and receiving the news that I was being recommended to a specialist was all the news I needed to hear to be certain that things were getting serious. My mammogram showed positive signs of abnormal breast tissue. My doctor explained to me that there was nothing more he could personally do, but to ensure that we moved forward as quickly as possible.

At that point, there was only one other person who was aware of what I was going through—my husband. His even-keeled outward personality cloaks the layers of worry he hides within. After discussing the possibilities, we decided it was best to think positive and wait. There was an uncomfortable silence at home for the rest of the evening as we both worried to ourselves.

The next few weeks took me on an emotional roller coaster. It was very difficult to focus on the day-to-day activities while I had the nagging thought of my specialist appointment on my mind. I kept teetering between telling myself that things would be just fine and trying to mentally prepare for the worst. I also started asking myself all the "hows."

How would I function in my day to day life?

How would I deliver the news to my family?

How would having cancer change my life?

How would getting a positive result affect all the plans that were already made for the year?

How? How? How? It was time to narrow the window of decisions. There were too many possibilities to consider and besides, nothing was certain. At least not yet because tomorrow is another day.

4

The Biopsy

As if the pandemic and the pending completion of treatment wasn't enough, my level of anxiety shot to the skies due to the civil unrest caused by the murder of George Floyd. I experienced an equally high level of fear for my fellow Black people and a high level of pride for the decision to stand up and fight! I could not bring myself to watch the horrific video. The look on that murderer's face and the reports of the screams for mercy from the victim that was reported, was enough to break my heart. Every single day that I woke up, I felt angry. Angry at the world for not protecting us. Angry at the world for their continued sub-human treatment and pretense of not knowing. I was also angry that all of our so-called "kitchen table talk" of things that we have had to experience and brush under the rug had to be discussed to prove many points.

Asides from being angry, I found myself feeling incredibly sad when thinking about the countless times I had been made to feel less than. I began to think about how differently my life was based on the country I lived in. Growing up in Jamaica, I didn't experience racism per-say for a few reasons. As a child in a country where the people were mostly Black, I was surrounded by people who looked like me. I saw people in successful positions who mirrored successes that I knew could be achieved. The country was not without its faults. Colorism was something I experienced, but it never made me feel as if I couldn't reach the heights of success. Spending the second part of my childhood in New York City was a shock! The racism was blatant. So blatant that my parents had to give me a crash course in how to survive at ten years old! Moving to Canada brought a new level of racism. This time, it came with a smile and a layer of politeness. I kept reminding myself of the backhanded compliments—many of them that ended with "for a Black person." There were countless times when I had to remind myself of that popular saying among the Black community of having to "work twice as hard to get half as much."

In Canada, racism whispers. In the United States, it screams.

I found myself resisting the urge to scroll through social media or to watch television. I was tired. I was exhausted. I needed to protect my mental health. While I was stuck indoors protecting both my physical and mental health, my fellow brothers and sisters were outdoors literally risking their lives in what could be considered our generation's civil rights movement. I cheered them on from afar and hoped and prayed that I wouldn't have to hear about other abuses being inflicted by bigots or by the systems that should have been protecting us. George Floyed did not die in vain. His murder catapulted a movement that will never be forgotten. His death forced change. It forced conversations among friends. It forced further corporate social responsibility and it forced us, as Black people, to know our voice and our dollars count!

Rest in Power.

So much to do, in so little time. I was so excited for this long-awaited vacation. Did I mention that in over five years, I had not been on a real vacation that required a flight? Sometimes it's hard for me to imagine that time flew by so quickly. We work so hard and we are always so focused on our "to-do" list that sometimes we forget to schedule fun. I do schedule fun on my calendar because I am quite the social butterfly, but this time fun was on my priority list.

My husband, my mother and I were embarking on our long awaited vacation in 4 days and we didn't even have our suitcases! We didn't have our Airbnb confirmed for our first stop! It was time for me to get it together. First things first—biopsy.

Shifting from tourism and hospitality to actual hospitals! What an interesting detour. I love hospitals! Everything about them is intriguing to me. I don't understand why most people get a weird feeling about them. Think about it … babies are born here. We come here for our healing and most times when we go in with despair, we leave with so much hope and rejuvenation. There was no getting away from this biopsy getaway. My experience was no different. I strolled in and they were kind and informative. The coolest part was getting to watch the entire thing play out. I got to watch on the screen as they extracted a total of 6 samples from two different areas of my right breast. It was an experience I will never forget. Another cool thing … it was truly a Canadian moment. There I was, a Black girl laying in “bed”, and being tended to by a male Sikh (turban in tow) and a female Muslim wearing a hijab. That moment made me smile and proud that I get to live in a country where this is the norm.

As I wrapped up the health component, I still had work and business tasks outstanding. I had a large event scheduled upon my return, so I had to ensure that all our marketing materials were scheduled to be deployed. The plan was to be on vacation and to work as little as possible. For the first time ever I planned on being unreachable. Now it was time to focus on being unreachable.

The suitcases were purchased and laying open, and still empty on the bedroom floor. I made the decision to take the day before my trip, off work, and I am so happy that I did. I could now focus on cleaning the house, finishing up the final event details for my business and completing packing my suitcases. I needed to play catch up with my mom who was packed days ago and to urge my husband to catch up because he had not started packing at all.

It was the day of our trip and I’m finally packed and ready to go!!! There were a few last minute items that needed to be taken care of. As I reflected on my lesson of the day—perspective—I prepared for some news. My first stop was to the specialist's office to receive the results of my biopsy. Based on the preliminary results without pathology, he determined I would be having a lumpectomy as soon as possible. Being the forward thinking person that I am, the first thing I said was, "Do I get new boobs?" His answer was no. My husband, being the serious person he is, did not find my question as amusing as the surgeon and I did. I figured it was the appropriate time to ask. When else would I get to ask for new boobs? Anyway, jokes aside, we had to plan. The surgeon was leaning toward the lump being cancerous. He wanted to move forward with the lumpectomy as it is the less invasive approach. Instead of removing all of my breast tissue, the surgeon planned on removing the tumors and a small amount of the tissue surrounding them. Our only hurdle was that I had a flight to catch that same evening and he was going on vacation in two weeks!

The surgeon and I went through our schedules thoroughly because he was adamant that this surgery was to take place before he went on vacation. As it stood, it was July 25th and his vacation was scheduled for August 9th. I wasn't scheduled to return from my vacation until August 5th. We settled on a surgery date of August 8th, the day before he was scheduled to leave. With that settled, I now had more things to add to my list before I could fully be in vacation mode.

I met with his nurses to go through questionnaires and paperwork relating to my surgery. I had to schedule a pre-operating visit with my General Practitioner. As I left the surgeon's office, I headed straight to my doctor's office to make an appointment and to fill them in on what had transpired since the last visit. With that out of the way, I headed to my hairdresser's because getting my hair done for my vacation was a must. I used this opportunity to make a mental note of what my next steps would be. I made a "need to know list" of people. Unfortunately, my family members were not on this list with the exception of my baby sister, who is a nurse. I filled her in, prior to the biopsy because she has the ability to be objective and to focus on the task at hand. I needed her to be my advocate and ensure that I was asking the right questions. I still had not told my middle sister or my mother, even though she was going on vacation with us.

There were only a few things left to wrap up now that my hair was looking great! I emailed the HR Manager at work and gave them the rundown of what I was facing. I left it up to them to bring my boss up to speed and notified them that I would only be back for a day and a half post vacation before I had to go into surgery. I updated my baby sister, swore my husband to secrecy, picked up dinner for my travel buddies, and headed home. That night, not a word about my pending surgery was discussed at the dining table. We were in full vacation mode. As I looked around, the house sparkled. There was an aroma of cleanliness mixed with the delightful smell of Jamaican food that made my soul blissful.

Wheels up! At about 11:50 pm we were off!!! It's official. We were on vacation! The three of us nestled together in our seats. My mom and husband dozed off and I was left to indulge in my vices ... watching movies and reading. Usually, I cannot sleep in transit so I knew I would need to entertain myself for this 7-hour flight. We landed at 11 am London time and tackled Heathrow Airport—the world's busiest international airport. We made our way through the masses, purchased passes for scenic Big Bus and the Thames river tours, bought an Oyster card to be used for the tube and hopped in the stereotypical black cab to make our way to our Airbnb. I must tell you that was the most expensive cab ride I have ever had to pay for. Eighty pounds later and only 30 minutes, we were at our destination. The cost hurt a bit more when we found out that we could've taken a train (tube) directly from the airport that would have cost us under four pounds! An expensive lesson learned for not wanting to pound the pavement.

Let's talk about accommodations. Our Airbnb was average. We found a 2 bedroom, 2 bathroom apartment in a middle class neighborhood on London's west end. It was close to all the amenities and had a bus stop right at the door. There were pubs within walking distance, trendy restaurants and a doorman to answer all our questions. The cost was more than I would like to discuss, but after hearing about the hotel conditions, I felt this was the best option. Coming from North America and knowing what to expect at a 5-star hotel would have you gob smacked in the UK. A 5-star here is equivalent to a 3-star in North America. The amenities are very limited and the cost is astronomical. Considering it was still early in the day and despite the fact that

I hadn't slept in about 26 hours, we decided to drop our stuff and begin exploring.

We opted to take the bus to a train station at Fulham Broadway. Our first stop was to a Portuguese chain restaurant called Nandos for some piri-piri deliciousness. I do know we have Nandos in Canada, but people have been raving about it here, so we thought we would give it a shot to see what the hype was about. Either it was no different or I was so hungry, it didn't even matter. Next stop was our first ride on the tube! We call it the subway in North America. I love using public transit in any city I visit. I love to people-watch and it's a safety in numbers thing. I don't like taking cabs or taxis as much because of my level of paranoia of getting in a car with a stranger. It should be no surprise that our first trip took us to the mall.

Westfield mall was a treat. It was an indoor/outdoor upscale mall like no other. We wanted an idea of retail prices in London as well as seeing what fashion items we could purchase. I love to shop so it was perfect except everything was incredibly expensive. I mean, there were shoes on sale at 50% off and still at sixty pounds!!! Shopping was not on the cards for me especially since I am still feeling the sting of that very expensive cab ride. The exhaustion from the last two days, the overwhelming feeling of my pending health condition and the enthusiasm of this vacation was starting to take a toll on me. I felt like a zombie. We headed back to our Airbnb to get some rest in anticipation of the next big day.

OOH LA LA PARIS!!! The city of lights will get a glimpse of my glow. Imagine not having slept for over 36 hours and then only having about 5 hours of it because I had to be up at 4:00 am!!! We are headed to Paris for a day trip. Thank God for the 24-hour tube service because we had to be at the main train station by 5:30 am. A family friend joined us on this trip as she served as our wonderful tour guide. Our package included our train ride to Paris, a metro pass and a boat tour down the river Seine. We got to the train station and checked in with our tour leader. My eyes lit up at the sight of Starbucks. Coffee was in my future! Still groggy and running on 5 hours of sleep over the past 48 hours would not deter me from the excitement of my first trip to Paris. As we waited for the train to board, we caught up with our family friend, grabbed more coffee and a hot breakfast sandwich from Pret a Manger—a UK staple.

A little over 2 hours later after leaving the St. Pancras station in London and traveling at about 150 km/hr under the English Channel, we arrived in Paris at the Gare du Nord. The first experience was a bit of a mess—our metro pass did not work and no one spoke English well enough to help us. Granted, we did not speak any French to help ourselves either. After about 30 minutes of trying to speak with many people, we finally found someone who helped us and got us all new passes. We were now off to see all that Paris had to offer!

We went looking for the iconic Eiffel Tower. As we roamed the cobbled streets of Paris in the direction of the tower, we were in admiration of the architecture of the buildings. Everything was so grand and so ornate. The buildings had character. We saw the river and knew we were headed in the right direction. We turned the corner and there she stood—the Eiffel Tower. To be honest, it was much smaller than I expected, but beautiful nonetheless. We walked through the crowds toward the tower to take a closer look at her magnificence. We opted not to take the ride to the top because we really wanted to maximize our day. Instead, we boarded our tour boat to get a majestic tour of the River Seine.

As we cruised along the river, there were larger than life buildings. I was in such awe of the Parisian architecture. Spending most of my life in North America got me used to a certain type of building facade, so you can imagine how awestruck I was. As we cruised past The Notre Dame, I was reminded of the fire that damaged a very large section of the historic gothic church earlier in the year. Even though a very large portion of the church was damaged, we still got to admire the majestic building. After looping back and getting off the cruise, we decided to go on a quest for nourishment. We wanted to find an idyllic Parisian café and experience some French dining. We found a café, but we didn't order anything that was traditionally French except the wine. I had pizza, yup! My husband, mother, and friend savored some rice bowls. Everything was delicious!

There were a couple of memorable moments aside from the ambiance and the food at Mokus. Their bathroom is a must-see. The stalls were unique. Each stall had a roll up garage-style door that was controlled by either a big green button to open or a big red button to close. The other memorable moment is a woman's worst nightmare. As we were all dining al fresco, a lady walked out of the restaurant in quite a hurry. The entire back of her dress was stuck inside her underwear—her red thong underwear! She was walking so quickly, that no one got a chance to stop her! Oh the embarrassment!

After the exquisite lunch and the impromptu peep show, we took a stroll to see the Arc de Triomphe and the Champs Elysées. It seemed like the perfect scene. The sky was blue, the sun was out and it looked like everything I expected Paris to be, so picturesque. After soaking it all in and visiting the Eternal Flame, we decided to take the metro and head over to the Louvre.

Paris is a very old city, so is its metro. Their ticketing system was antiquated, especially when comparing it to the much older tube system in London. Before visiting Europe, NYC was the bar! A very high bar at that. The subway runs 24 hours per day and spans the entire city. You had no need for a car as you could get anywhere using transit.

The Louvre is massive! The building was magnificent. I would have loved to have had the time to walk the entire museum, but that has to be saved for another day. The magnitude of all the buildings is still astonishing to me. I keep trying to imagine how these buildings were built back in those time periods with less machinery. They all look like they were built to last. Built with precision. Built with care.

Now the only thing left for me to find in Paris was a typical Parisian bakery. As a food connoisseur when I think French, I think pastries. After a lot of walking in circles and with time dwindling down to catch our train back to London, we ended up having to purchase French macarons from a kiosk at the train station. Twenty thousand steps later, we finished our day tour of the City of Lights and boarded our train to head back to London—the City of Dreams.

Reflecting on this week really puts a lot of things in perspective for me. I can either dwell on the bad news that was delivered or focus on the fact that I have a vacation that many are not blessed to experience. I chose to live in the moment and focus on all the positive things in life. I could enjoy some of the world's most beautiful places with my husband and my mother. I was given the gift of hope by my surgeon. I also realized how much I trusted and valued the opinion of experts. I didn't spend my time worrying about the pending surgery because I trusted in what I was being told by my surgeon. I trusted that he was knowledgeable and that he would make the best decision for me and my health. Tomorrow is going to be a new day.

I was a tourist on a mission. Admittedly, I have a love affair with food. I have a unique superpower of being able to remember where I have had "the best" of any food item I have eaten. I still remember the first time I tasted some delicious lemon tea biscuits that were gifted to me. They were from Harrods. These were extra thin, crispy, melt-in-your-mouth kind of shortbread biscuits. They left a tingling in your mouth and a refreshing taste of lemon. The perfect balance. I always promised myself that if I ever got the chance, I would try to find those biscuits. So off to Harrods we went in search of those memorable sweet treats. Walking from the tube station to Harrods was a sight to see. It was like walking down 5th Avenue in NYC. The opulence, the wealth, the clothes, the cars, the everything that was out of my price range. It prepared me for Harrods.

Once we arrived in Harrods, I was lost in the gloriousness of it all. I didn't know if I should look to the left or right. Even the staircase was a sight to behold. It wasn't just a high-end department store; it was a tourist attraction. Maneuvering from floor to floor on the Egyptian Staircase and admiring all the high-end clothes, shoes, and accessories along with the other patrons, was mind blowing. There were no prices on the tags and you know what that means; if you have to ask the price, you cannot afford it. Having flashbacks of that 80-pound cab ride led me to the gift store section of this massive attraction to search for my cookies. Unfortunately, I did not get lucky. I did purchase some shortbread cookies to make up for my time. We decided to splurge and get our lunch from the food hall before heading out. It was worth every penny.

The highlight of today was reconnecting with my cousin. I have a cousin who was named after me and is two years younger. We haven't seen each other since I was ten! It just so happens that after he completed his studies in Jamaica, he moved to London. Somehow, my mother got in contact with him and we all agreed to meet up at one of London's many museums. Oh! Did I mention that all museums in London are pay-what-you-can? Be still my heart! Ok, I need to focus. We walked up to this museum, which made me feel like I was about to walk onto the Harry Potter set. It was grand. It was ornate. It was the Natural History Museum. As we waited outside the museum's entrance, I looked up to find my cousin strolling up with the biggest smile ever! This made my day more than he could ever know. I am big on family and I like to know that my family members are just a phone call or text message away. As he walked up with his daughter, it felt magical. For my mother, this was an even more special moment as she had never met her nephew before. I could see the joy in her eyes! We were so happy to be able to be around each other that we just couldn't stop looking at each other and smiling. Talk about making history at the Natural History Museum.

He took us on a mini tour of Central London. We walked along Oxford Street and shopped for souvenirs. Walking down Oxford Street reminds me of a cross between Canal Street in NYC and Disney World. Picture jam packed stores with so many items that they spill out to the sidewalk and endless types of souvenirs. T-shirts, shot glasses, purses, magnets, everything. You name it, they have it. We drove around and he pointed out things along the way and gave us some true nontourist insights about living in London. We also took a stroll and found a quintessential pub and finally got to try some traditional pub food. I AM IN LOVE WITH CHIPS! Period. How is it that I have never had this before? It's the perfect thickness, saltiness, and crispiness. I can't go back to regular fries after this.

That day was everything I could dream of. A fun day with family. A bond was re-formed. I can't wait to see what the future holds for all of us, but I guarantee that it won't be another twenty-eight years before we see each other again.

Family over everything.

We started our day on a river boat tour of the Thames. Before I got on the boat, I got to soak in Westminster Abbey. I love buildings with such detail and grandeur. I almost didn't notice Big Ben because it was covered in scaffolding and only one face was visible. Westminster Abbey made up for that. The river tour gave us a chance to see both historic and modern sides of Central London. I was enamored by Tower Bridge and the London Eye. It felt like a scene from James Bond. The juxtaposition of a historical building like the Westminster Abbey on one side of the river and the modern London Eye on the other was a perfect representation of how the past and the present can coexist in harmony.

We continued our day with the hop-on, hop-off Big Bus double decker tour. I must also point out that today was the first hot and sunny day that we experienced since our arrival. Now that's a treat in London because London weather is mostly gloomy. You know what that means … break out the dresses! Our first hop off spot was at Buckingham Palace. It was as grand as one would imagine. The gates were adorned in gold, the guards were standing at attention and there was the large Queen Victoria statue, perfect for photo ops. The Queen was not on site.

The next stop was Kensington Palace. It was not as grand as Buckingham Palace. I made a mistake and thought it was the workers quarters. As we continued to walk around, my mom asked a lady to identify the palace. To our surprise we were looking at it. It was still large, but it did not have the same effect as Buckingham Palace. It was surrounded by a beautiful park and lovely gardens. We strolled around and soaked up the sun. We hopped back on the bus to take in the sights such as Piccadilly Circus and Trafalgar Square. It seems we chose the perfect day for sight-seeing because the next day was dreary.

Rain, rain go away. It was like a monsoon out there. It rained nonstop for hours and gave us a chance to relax a bit. We decided to run across the street to a local pub for lunch and it was a treat! Our meals were less than six pounds each and we got paninis with chips—my newfound love. We ate and soaked up the scenery of people passing by as if the rain had no impact on their day. I guess this was typical weather for them. After our meals, we went back to our dry, comfortable Airbnb. As the evening approached, the rain finally decided to ease up, so we met a friend at the other Westfield Mall—this one in East London.

This mall was just as opulent as the previously visited Westfield Mall on the West End. It was next to Queen Elizabeth Olympic Park. I have never been in a mall that had restaurants in their food court that offered happy hour at a very large bar and had an extensive menu. We ate at a Brazilian restaurant that provided a memorable meal. This was our last night in London and I must admit, I cannot wait to return.

Before we left, we tried to fit in another full day of touring. Imagine the irony. We had a traditional English breakfast at a French café in the heart of Chinatown in London, England. Baked beans, tomatoes, eggs, sausage, and toast. We strolled around Chinatown to see all the shops and decorative details. It was a beautiful ending to our London adventures.

After a quick trip on the tube to the airport only costing us about three pounds and not the 80 pounds we spent upon arrival, we were off to our next destination. We had a layover in Brussels that gave us a Home Alone moment. Picture us running through the airport as we had to catch our connecting flight from the end of one terminal to the other end of the airport. We made it in the nick of time. We landed in Madrid at about 11:45 pm and made a quick exit to get a taxi to our Airbnb. What a difference a country made! For a fraction of the cost of what we paid in London, we got a 2 bedroom, 2 bathroom, penthouse, two floor apartment in the heart of the city. It came with a rooftop patio and all the amenities one could need.

Our gracious host waited for our arrival and showed us the ropes. We decided to venture out into the night to find food and to see what Madrid had to offer. People were out walking their dogs, headed out to bars or just going out for a stroll. It reminds me of life in Jamaica; one of leisure. Not even a block away was a 24-hour pizza restaurant with a constant flow of patrons. Our pizza options were impressive. For as little as two and half euros, we could get a slice with all the goodies! No basic pepperoni here. We took our slices, went back to our new home, ate and got ready for what the next day would bring.

Our first full day in Madrid was a dream. The weather was a sunny 36 degrees Celsius with very little humidity. We strolled around our new neighborhood to discover it was filled with restaurants of all kinds, boutiques, supermarkets, souvenir shops, casinos, and more. You can find everything your heart desires within a few blocks. We decided to mirror our choice of a bus tour just as we did in London. This time we got a 2-day tour.

Spanish architecture is something to be admired. Everything looked clean, white, deliberately placed, and larger than life. One sculpture in particular was captivating and was on temporary display. It stood about 12 meters high in the Plaza de Colon. It is titled Julia. A clean, simple, all white but detailed sculpture of a woman's head in the middle of the square. Striking and beautiful, Julia was a sculpture created by Barcelona born artist Juame Plensa.

After their afternoon siestas, in the evenings, Madrid came alive with fiestas. As we disembarked our bus tour for the day and grabbed a bite for supper, we explored Madrid on foot. People started pouring out onto the streets. We noticed that retail stores were open pretty late—some until 11 pm! As the streets came alive, so did the squares. It seemed as though the squares were the meeting points for nightly entertainment. We saw dancers, singers, and other performance artists. We saw people selling their souvenirs and counterfeit merchandise. It looked like a scene you would expect at a street festival in the middle of the day but instead, this was at night! I felt like I was dreaming.

Day 2 in Madrid was no different than day 1 weather-wise. We continued our bus tour adventure and got off to explore the Palace Royale. If I thought Buckingham Palace was grand and ostentatious, then I stand corrected. This palace dwarfed it! It was massive! The gardens were lush, the buildings were ornate, and everything was immaculate. We spent the better part of 1 hour exploring the garden and admiring the exterior of the palace. We then took a stroll to find a historical church with a museum; the Museum of the Almudena Cathedral. The museum is dedicated to the history of the church in Madrid. It had beautiful mosaics, sculpture, and historical objects. Did I mention how much I love museums? I also love ornate churches. We walked around and learned about the history of the church. I was baptized Catholic but I have never considered myself one. I do like learning about how different countries and cultures view religion and how it has impacted their history. Catholicism has had a huge impact on Spanish culture. This church is the first Catholic Church to be consecrated outside of Rome. It is considered the most religious building in Madrid.

We hopped back on the bus to take in more of the sights of Madrid. We explored the financial district, and got to drive by the epic Real Madrid Football Stadium. If you are a fan of football, then you know how big of a deal the Real Madrid Football Club is. The stadium gave me chills and all I kept thinking was, *I wish*

I could experience a match in this space! We ended our tour by exploring an outdoor market close to one of the museums. We soaked up the sun and definitely revisited what the nightlife had to offer before retreating for the night. Tomorrow was yet another day.

It was all about museum day. Madrid has over 20 museums, so it was hard to choose! It is a dream for a museum lover like myself. We visited three museums. My most memorable of the three was the National Archeological Museum. I could have spent days there. This was the museum that had an extensive area dedicated to Christianity.

I also experienced the cleanest subway system I have ever taken. Navigating the system to purchase a subway pass was quite interesting and it challenged my comprehension of Spanish. The subway system itself was easy to navigate. The first museum was one dedicated to fine art. It was an adventure in itself to find the museum. You wouldn't believe that we walked around for about 30 minutes, just to find out that the museum was a mere 50 steps away from where we were initially.

We then went to a contemporary art museum that looked like it was housed in a fort. The third museum we visited was the National Archeological Museum. It was the first museum I have ever visited that had an entire section dedicated to Christianity. There were detailed crosses of varying sizes, different Bibles, thrones, and robes. It was obvious how much Christianity was deeply rooted in the history of Spain. It felt good to take a few hours to learn about the country we were visiting.

That was our final full day in Madrid. I am definitely going to miss the great weather, great food, cheap wine, and the vibe. This place really made its mark on me. I could pick up my life and move here with very little hesitation. They are culturally rich and full of tradition. They also know how to celebrate life.

We roamed the streets and landed on a tapas bar that served the best sangria I have ever had. I pride myself on my sangria making skills. I am usually the one bringing a bucket or two to a party. I took one sip of the white sangria and vowed to work on my recipe. The red sangria was delightful as well. I could've stayed at that bar and drank sangria all day. What a great way to end a trip. Something tickling my taste buds.

5

The Surgery

My first day of the radiation process—I see an end in sight. Walking into a new wing of the hospital brought a new level of curiosity. At Credit Valley Hospital, the radiation wing has a feeling of being in an ark. Think Noah building an ark in 2020 with wood and glass. It doesn't have that hospital feel one would expect. It is quite relaxing as I am surrounded by sunshine and green plants. As the nurse explains the entire treatment process to me, I am very much aware that I am embarking on a new journey with all new experiences. I listen intently to their instructions of what to do each day upon my arrival, what ointments I will need for my skin, and what to expect in terms of wait times on treatment days. I am a woman of order and structure and going through the cancer treatment process was filled with structure.

Before even starting that first treatment, I was already dreaming of what my new normal would be post-treatment. Imagining the vacations I would like to take, the joy of eating meals when my taste buds are back to normal, hanging out with family and friends, enjoying glasses of wine, and just living life. As I walk into the changing room, and change into the gown, I am ready to once again embark upon a new part of this journey of life. To think that this all started months ago with one lump!

Adios España! Hello reality! We strolled out of our Airbnb at 5 am with our suitcases in tow. Party-goers were on their way home and the street was still awake. We made our way to the airport and embarked on our 8-hour journey home.

As soon as we landed, the reality of the Monday blues hit us. Our phones were all abuzz. I was still trying to hold on to the feeling of being on vacation while knowing that I would have to break some bad news to my mother within an hour. As we got our luggage and boarded our taxi to head home, we got a message from my godmother in Jamaica to call my uncle urgently. These types of messages are never good. As we pulled up to our house, my mom got on the phone and spoke to my uncle. While she was doing that, I was busy trying to figure out the best way to deliver my news to her. Instead, she came in and filled us in about how my uncle's entire leg was swollen and he was undergoing tests.

They thought it was a side effect from a surgery he had a few years ago. With that worry in her heart, I still knew I had to deliver the second most difficult news I have ever had to give her. The first was when I was in high school and my uncle called me and told me of my grandmother's passing. I still remember how difficult that was for us to deal with. For this one, I just said it as directly as I could.

"Mommy, I am having surgery on Thursday and there's a high possibility that it is breast cancer."

I had to explain that I went through all the tests without her knowledge and that I knew all this before we went on vacation and that there was no way I was going to allow this news to ruin our time together. The look on her face is something I will never forget as long as I live. My mother has a hard outer shell, but she worries a lot—like any mother would. She held back tears. She stood firmly and said she will be there on Thursday and let's just get it done. She understood there was nothing that she could do except be positive and pray. She understood that I didn't want to make a huge deal of it. She understood. That was what I needed to hear.

While my husband drove my mother home, I decided to go to the supermarket and call my sisters on the way. My baby sister was involved in the entire process so I only needed to get my middle sister up to speed. I dreaded this almost as much as I dreaded telling my mom. My middle sister is the one with all the emotions. My family was full of surprises today because they both took the news better than I could have ever imagined. After delivering the news to both my mother and my middle sister, I called my baby sister and looped her in on how well everyone took the news. She was just as surprised and relieved as I was.

The fridge was full of groceries and my suitcases were unpacked. I read through all the paperwork provided to me by the surgeon for the big day. I was heading to the office for 7 am followed by all my pre-op activities. Enough of planning for the future, I got some curried chicken in my belly because this is the longest I have ever gone in my life without Jamaican food—almost two weeks! The food I had on vacation was delicious but nothing beats some good home cooking. I was full, I had a great vacation, I checked all my "to-do list" for the day. It was time to rest.

Early wake ups are no good when you haven't done it in a long time. Imagine going to work post vacation and everyone wants to know how your vacation was, while you try to focus on getting as much work done in a day and a half. Four hundred emails later and only 4 hours to get through them I finally wrapped up my day at 11 am. Before I could head out, I had to have a tough meeting with my boss to deliver the bad news. One of those, "Hello, vacation was great but I am going to be off for a minimum of four weeks starting on Thursday". The meeting went as well as one could have imagined. There was no stress. Work would continue with or without me. It was time to take care of myself.

Pre-op was interesting. I checked in and waited about an hour for a nurse. She went through a detailed questionnaire and reviewed everything in my take home package. I had blood work done and then took off to visit my family doctor to get his blessings and signature for the surgery. One more full day before I could get this cancer out.

It was hump day, the day before "removing the lump" day! I didn't have to get to the office until 9 am. The long to-do list had to be tackled, but what didn't get done would have to wait. What I didn't look forward to was having to deliver the news to some of my colleagues. I must admit, some of them made it easy for me because of their personalities. We managed to find ways to joke about the entire situation—especially the way in which I delivered the news. I was very nonchalant and I definitely did not sugar-coat anything. We talked about how I found out and how I was feeling about the entire situation, but for the most part, the conversations were easier than anticipated.

It was about 3 pm and I was finally able to gather my entire team in one room. I haven't seen two of the three team members since before my vacation so I used a few minutes to let them know how it went. I then had to tell them that I was going to be out of office for a while. When I delivered my "why", the entire feeling in the room changed. Let me paint you a picture of the personalities in the room. There is me, who really doesn't get emotional or likes to deal with emotional situations. There is one person who is always happy. She has an extroverted personality and is always ready to dance, sing, and just laugh. There is a second person who is even-keeled. She is a bit high strung, and has a great personality that you will only get to know if she feels comfortable with you. The third person is the one who balances the group. He is very caring and considerate. Sometimes quiet and yet funny. He always wants to ensure that everyone around him was feeling great and safe.

Imagine how I was feeling as I watched them all react to my news. I feel my job as the head of my department is to teach, guide, uplift, and protect my team. I was now the one who needed to feel uplifted and assured that everything was going to work out and be just fine. They wanted to react, but also understood that I didn't like having to handle emotional situations. I saw them fight back tears. I saw them look down and look everywhere in the room but at me because they just didn't want to break down. Somehow, they found the strength to reassure me that it would be ok. They knew that the reassurance I needed wasn't that I was going to be ok, it was that they were going to make it work without me. That they would put forth their best in my absence so that I wouldn't have to worry about them. They knew what my concerns were and I am thankful that they understood that I would take care of myself as long as they made me feel like I would be comfortable enough to walk away without being too concerned. We reviewed a few items that I wanted to get out of the way, we all embraced and wished each other well. I hope they understood how much I appreciated them and how much their reassurance was helping me push through the day.

My work day wasn't quite complete. I delivered the news to one more person, who did start to tear up so I had to walk away. I was determined not to cry and I knew I had to remove myself from the scenario. Once things settled down, we had a quick chat and called it a day. Later in the afternoon, I received a phone call, and was told to come outside. As I walked out of my office into the parking lot, who did I see but a couple of my besties with their kids. They put together the sweetest gift basket of items that I would need over the coming days. Their daughters each made me a card echoing well wishes and love. If I had any doubts about what was to come, they were immediately erased because I knew I had the power of love, well-wishes, and positivity on my side. My day at work could not have ended any better.

There was one pit-stop before heading home—I had to part with my nails. I had to get them cut and the polish removed. One quick trip to the nail salon and a quick explanation to my manicurist and I was ready to go.

We made the decision to move into my mother's place for a couple of weeks as I recuperated. This would give me all the love and support I needed in order to heal properly and be surrounded by family. Once again, the suitcase and I were one. As soon as it was unpacked, it was time to pack it again. So many things were on my mind. I had no idea how I would feel after surgery so I didn't know what to prepare for. I found all the comfy dresses I could find, and grabbed a pair of sweatpants. That was really only a total of about 3 dresses. I had pajamas, a book, my laptop, pillows, a comfy blanket, and that's all she wrote. I ate my last meal of the night and for the next day planned to wear a long black sleeveless cotton dress along with my flip-flops. I packed my backpack with my paperwork and ID, jumped in the shower, and washed my hair as part of the pre-op requirements. I was ready for the next day. It was going to be my Grey's Anatomy Day.

The big day arrived. I woke up, took a shower, and had to remember not to wear any jewelry. I must admit, I thought I would feel very nervous as it was my first major surgery, but I was surprisingly calm. I got to the hospital promptly at 6:40 am with my husband and mother to walk with me through this journey. I checked in and changed into the ever so stylish hospital gown. We ran through the hospital patient update system which enabled them to receive notifications for each step of the process. We reviewed all the documentation with the nurse and sat in the waiting room making the best of our morning.

After about half an hour of waiting my limo in the form of a wheelchair arrived. Admittedly, I was very excited to get a wheelchair ride! They looked so comfy and as I sank in the seat, it felt as comfortable as it looked. By this time, my husband had to run off to get a few hours in the office as he was still playing catch up from being on vacation. This left my mom and me to continue the adventure. Our next stop was to get a preoperative ultrasound. This one is a more detailed ultrasound than the ones I did in the past. It was over an hour of scans. They also had to inject a fluorescent fluid in my breast and image the path it took to my lymph nodes. This apparently would help guide the surgeons so that they would know what nodes to remove for the biopsy in order to help assess the stage of the cancer. I wonder if I was glowing like the Pandoran Syaksuks of Navi' in Avatar! It's funny how you don't think of these processes unless you are going through them. Luckily for me, I am quite curious, so I asked questions about every step of the way. After the ultrasound, it was time for a wheelchair trip to adventure number two!

Imagine a six inch wire hanging out of your body. Imagine it was put there on purpose. Imagine being awake and watching it all happen. Pretty cool huh? At least that's what I thought after it was done. The nurse and I kept joking about me wearing a wire. The doctor inserted a wire that went straight through the actual tumor. It served as a guide for the surgeon so that he knew exactly what area to focus on during surgery. Then I was off to my next stop!

If you were uncomfortable about the last stop, imagine doing a mammogram with a wire inserted in your breast. It was a "gentle" mammogram, and yet a bit awkward and unnerving. I didn't feel a thing because the entire area was numb, but just the thought of my breast being compressed with a wire hanging out of it was not an easy one. I made it through and was whisked off to the pre-surgery area. Once there, the nurse gave me a couple of slow activating pain killers that would activate post-surgery. This was really my first meal of the day—two tablets and a shot of good old fashioned water. At this point, it was about 12:15 pm. I had spent over 5 hours in the hospital and was ready to get started.

The waiting area for the surgery was interesting. The surgeon's name was on a wall and there were two chairs in front of it along with a curtain. My mother and I waited in this area as we watched other families wait in their assigned areas. I was interviewed by the surgeon again and he answered all my questions regarding post-surgery activities. The surgery would be performed on my right breast and arm area and he encouraged me to use my right arm and to try to be active after surgery. He reassured us that it was a straightforward surgery and that he saw it going very well. He proceeded to mark "X" all over my right arm and shoulder so that everyone was on the same page in the operating room about what side they were working on. I then met the other surgeon who asked me another list of questions and reassured me of the process. The anesthesiologist was next. She verified that I didn't have anything to eat except for the 2 tablets, that we will pretend were eggs, and my shot of water, that we can say was my tequila. She let me know that she is the person in control of the operating room and that she will ensure that everything goes smoothly. It was time to part ways with my mother as it was time for me to continue on this journey on my own. Along with my couture hospital gown, I was donned in my fancy foot cover and head cover and sashayed down the hallway with a nurse toward the operating room.

This part threw me in a loop. I never imagined that I would walk into an operating room. That's not how it happens in Grey's Anatomy. I had this expectation of being wheeled in on a gurney with my IV already in and nurses around me reassuring me that it was going to be just fine. To add to the drama of it all, I imagined the hallway lined with nurses cheering me on into surgery, and once getting into the room, looking up at the gallery of residents eager to see what was on the agenda for the day. Now that I was out of TV land, I could tell you that it did NOT happen that way.

As I strolled with the lovely nurse toward the door of the operating room, I shared my Grey's Anatomy vision. She opened the door and BOOM! There was the table and another nurse. As I strolled in, I politely acclaimed that the room was insanely cold and also told them not to worry about me because I was sure I wouldn't be able to feel anything in a few minutes because I would be "knocked out cold." The other nurses in the room got a chuckle and they guided me to lay on the operating table. I am not a small woman. This table looked like I would've rolled right off if I had a bad dream. As I climbed on and centered myself, I put my arms out and felt a bit like Jesus on the cross. The surgeon came into the room and reviewed the case once more so that everyone was on the same page prior to surgery. The last thing I remember is a cold fluid running through my left arm, a mask over my face, the nurse telling me to take deep breaths, and me happily singing, "Don't worry, about a thing. Cause every little thing is gonna be alright"—my favorite Bob Marley song in my head.

I woke up many hours later in a bed in a recovery area. To be honest, my recollection of the first recovery area is blurry. I do remember a nurse waking me up and constantly asking how I was feeling. I remember being in and out of "sleep" about thrice before being given a tiny shot glass or medicine cup worth of crushed ice—my tequila on the rocks. I was awake enough to ask the nurse for a Dixie cup size of crushed ice because my throat was insanely dry. That's when I realized I was intubated during the surgery. The nurse gave me the additional cup of ice and wheeled me to the secondary recovery area so that my family could see me.

In this area, they would only allow one family member at a time. My mom came in first to see how I felt. Again, I can barely remember that conversation. Partly because those ice cubes tasted like sushi rolls and partly because I was still trying to wake up. She then switched places with my husband. I do remember him chuckling and it was probably because I was still loopy from the anesthesia. I remember the nurse going down a list of dos and don'ts post-surgery. The highlight of that conversation was when she mentioned the most appetizing word I heard all day—POPSICLE!!! At this point, I hadn't eaten anything in almost 24 hours so a popsicle sounded like a filet mignon to me. In true fashion, I requested a red popsicle and believe me when I say, I can still taste it on my tongue.

The next step in this process was to get dressed and to blow this popsicle stand. As my husband started to help me get dressed, I realized how fragile I really was. It was a challenge to navigate my body knowing that I had large bandages covering my right breast, under my right arm and below my right shoulder blade. There was also a drainage tube that hindered my motion. When I finally got dressed, a couple of sweet volunteers took me on my final limo wheelchair ride of the day—out to the parking lot. I suddenly became very aware of every movement in my body.

Every step I took was intentional. Getting into the car was done with precision as I had to try to angle myself in the back seat so that I would be comfortable for a 40+-minute ride that would not interfere with my surgical wounds and would allow quick access to my barf bag. Half-way into the ride, I became insanely nauseous. I had to ride the balance of the trip with a plastic bag to my mouth.

We finally arrived at my mother's house and I parked myself on the couch. My husband made a trip to the pharmacy to pick up my prescription of Percocet® and some extra strength Tylenol®. Somehow he purchased a 100 tablet bottle! Who needed that many pain killers? It was best if I didn't speak too soon. Perhaps I would need those. I had dinner and a Percocet® and off to bed I went.

Have you ever tried sleeping on your back, while there is a tube jutting out of it? I don't recommend it. We packed a few pillows behind me so that I could sleep upright. I discovered that sleeping flat on my back would not only hurt the area where the drain port was located, but would also hurt my breast due to the position it would rest in. I also couldn't sleep on my left side, because of the way my breast would "hang" to the left. Obviously, I couldn't sleep on my right side or on my stomach. Throughout the night and much throughout the day during naps, we would toy around with different degrees of inclination for my back, to see what would work. No level of inclination worked better than the next. I just had to understand that I would be perpetually tired and had to try to survive on naps throughout this difficult time.

My family took care of me hand and foot to ensure that I would relax and not do too much. Quite frankly, I wasn't allowed to do anything except watch TV! Netflix became my best friend in between my naps. I started watching Schitt's Creek to add some humor to my day. I wanted to absorb as much joy, laughter and positivity throughout the healing process. I also wanted to become conscious of my thoughts. I was intentional about dismissing any negativity and focusing my thoughts on positive outcomes.

The past few days felt much the same. The same lack of sleep, pain, and foggy memory. I found it difficult to piece together some details of the past few days. I tried to add tidbits of normalcy to my day, but it was hard. Everyone wanted me to rest, and I did feel exhausted. I would have, however, loved to have a chore to do, so that I didn't have to sit all day. As much as I said that, I felt like I needed a nap. I had great intentions, but I really did need to focus on rest, recovery, and restoration.

I still felt like my memory was a blur. As I tried to remember the simplest of details over the past few days, it was challenging. I had been trying to focus on recalling some of the missing information. It was already daunting to know that I missed a few hours of my life due to surgery, but to still have fuzzy moments was just frustrating and scary.

The following day was self-proclaimed Family Fun Day! There was an overload of emotions, but it was all worth it. It was a full house—my mom, husband, both nephews, both sisters, and in-laws were present. If you didn't think that was enough pandemonium, we were having a dinner party too! My cousin, who we had met while on vacation in London, was now on our turf for his vacation. He was coming over with his cousin from the other side of the family and his sister. It was nice to have the focus off of me for a while. They did not know about the surgery. My mom shared it with them when they came in, but I was so happy that there wasn't a big deal made of it. There was a small and graceful moment of empathy, and we shifted quickly to enjoy the day.

A day later, I had my first visit to the clinic to get my dressing changed. I didn't know what to expect. It would also be my first car ride, or trip outside the home since the surgery. I missed the little things in life. There were so many things I took for granted like being able to drive. Donned in one of my limited edition dresses due to the restrictions of what I could wear, I felt giddy as I got into the car. I was so excited to be out of the house even if it was for a visit to get my dressing changed but my attire had to be strategic. First of all, I needed to wear flip-flops as it was easy to get my feet in and out of them. I only wore strapless dresses, as it was difficult to find ones with sleeves that didn't interfere with the bandages under my arms. I also had to ensure that the dress either had extra material on the top or was loose. I could not wear a bra and I also didn't want to wear anything that was too restricting. We are not told how to prepare for moments like these.

As we made our way to the clinic, I paid attention to every detail on our ride. It was as if I didn't know if I would be able to experience being outside again. I knew it would be about another three days before I would be able to enjoy this again, so even if it was something as mundane and annoying as just the traffic, I was determined to enjoy it. As we approached the clinic, it dawned on me that I didn't know what I was getting into. I had no idea what to expect.

As the nurse removed the first bandage, I felt the nervousness. I couldn't see the scar on my breast, but I didn't want to see it either. This was the first time I didn't want to watch the process. It would have made it too real for me. He changed the dressing under my arm and measured the amount of waste collected from my drain tube. This drain tube was another hindrance. It was connected to a plastic bulb, shaped like a grenade that collected the fluid from my body. I always had to have it pinned to my clothing and it posed a problem with mobility. I knew I couldn't wait for it to be removed. I had to keep track of the amount of fluid collected each day and they would remove it once there was a consistent number over a period of two days. The nurse completed the dressing change, wiped down areas of my skin that was still covered in the antiseptic used during surgery and called it a day.

While leaving the clinic, I felt a bit more refreshed. It had been really hard to feel completely clean as I was only allowed to take baths and I could not get the bandages or dressings wet. They were more like sponge baths. I also had to learn to do basic tasks with my left hand as I was right-handed. Some basic tasks seemed daunting to perform, but it gave me some challenges to overcome throughout my day. On the positive side, I was getting adept at becoming ambidextrous. These active experiences were a welcoming interlude to the mundane moments of sitting passively on the couch and watching television.

The day after was not much different from any other. I woke up, had breakfast, sat on the couch, napped, had lunch, napped, had dinner, napped, and then went to bed for a deeper nap. Really! That is what my days looked like. However, I made a deliberate choice to be grateful for them and decided to appreciate them. I looked back and reflected on how my life was as early as a month ago, and realized that I wouldn't allow myself to nap even if I needed to. I considered napping as being lazy. I was a workaholic and now I had to become accustomed to being what I would typically consider idle. I realized that I would often ask myself why I couldn't take some time to myself and relax more. Sometimes it takes going through a traumatic experience in order to value the time you have in the body you have been blessed with. We take this and so much more for granted. This was my opportunity to finally find the work-life balance that we often search for in our lives. It was then that I decided I was going to relax and savor every minute of it.

A new day leads to new experiences and this time, I had visitors! It was great to have a visit from a friend. We sat and talked for hours. We kept the surgery talk to a minimum and I was thankful. I wanted to have some normalcy during our visit.

I wanted to know what was going on in the world. This might have been my FOMO—Fear of Missing Out moment. It was a good moment to shift my focus from the outside cacophony to the inner stillness of my being.

Once again, I was taking the time to reflect. It had almost been a week since my surgery and my family and friends had bent over backward to make sure that my healing journey was not going to be arduous. They made sure I was comfortable, that I was taking the time to relax. I was also trying to make a huge decision for my business. I had two events planned for the next month. One event was only a week away. The other was in September. I had to decide if I would be canceling the September event. It would be the first time in seven years that this event would not go on. I would have to make a decision by the end of the week but for now, I was focused on making next week's event a success.

It was a week since my surgery and the day of my second appointment with the nurse to get my dressing changed. I would love to say that one week makes a world of a difference, but it would not be true. I was still groggy, missing bits of information, and still in pain even though the day was spent relaxing on the couch and watching Schitt's Creek on Netflix. Not wanting to become dependent on any of the medication prescribed to me, I tried not to focus on the pain or discomfort.

If I was being honest, the most discomforting part of these days aside from sleeping was using the bathroom and bathing with the drain tube attached. The tube made it incredibly difficult to maneuver or complete the simplest of tasks. My hope was to have this tube removed as soon as possible. Each day as I drained the line, I recorded the amount of fluid collected in the grenade looking pouch. Finally, during my routine trip to get my dressing changed, the nurse said what I was longing to hear. She decided it was time to remove the pouch.

Remember, this pouch was attached to my body via a tube that was inside my skin and held in place by surgical stitches. The nervousness began to build because I do not have a high pain tolerance. As I lay on my left side on the clinic table, the nurse began cutting the stitches that held the tube in my body. I had to remember to breathe because naturally, I tend to hold my breath during stressful moments. My husband was holding my hand and supporting me through what seemed like an hour-long process. To be honest, it had to be less than 2 minutes. All I felt was warm fluid rolling down my back as the nurse said, “It’s out.” Sweet relief! I would now have a better range of motion.

The final two days at my mom’s house were restful. They were much the same as other days. Naps, television and delicious food. It seemed like I was living my life on autopilot. I did, however, miss being home. It was almost a whole month away from home and I had only slept in my bed for just two nights during that period. I also missed being alone. I enjoy alone time, I enjoy solitude. It is therapeutic. In times like these it also allows for reflection and for some realization. As my husband and I geared up to go home, there was still one thought on my mind ... *I had an event to host in a few days.*

As I arrived home with Tupperware filled with lots of food in tow, I felt a new form of appreciation. It was nice to have family and friends who love and support us in times of need. It was also nice to have a space that allows us to just be and appreciate that alone time to reflect. Unfortunately, the reflection had to wait. In four days, I had to be ready to host a full scale business seminar.

In the spirit of taking it easy, I made a game plan with my event planner and some friends. Event day had to go off without a glitch and I also didn't want anyone outside of my inner-circle to know about my surgery just yet. With the help of my friends, we decided it would be best not to make the announcement regarding my health at the event. The announcement needed to be tied into an action for everyone to take—aside from sending me well wishes. Let's focus on the event first. I spent the next few days slowly getting things in order for the event so that things would go smoothly and without any pressure. Self-care was my focus.

It was the morning of the event and as I rose, anxiety set in as I needed to have my energy level at 100% for the entire day. So far, since the surgery, I had not made it through the day without an afternoon siesta and today would be the first sans siesta. My husband packed the car and we headed out. At the venue, my mother, the event planners, and my friends were ready to get the ball rolling. The plan was for me to do as little as possible while they managed the set-up. Within the first hour of the day, everything was set up for our guests. Our vendors were in place, and it was show time.

Let me give you a synopsis of what our seminars are like. Typically, we choose an elaborate banquet hall for this leg of our event. This particular one serves as our home-coming event because it is hosted in Mississauga—the city where the business was founded. It will always have a special place in my heart. The event comprised of vendors, guest speakers and of course, guests. As our guests started to arrive, it was finally time. I was ready to try to give it my all for the next 8 hours of the day. I smiled, greeted guests, introduced speakers to the stage, had lunch, shook hands, and laughed quite a bit throughout the day. I had a lot of support with me and was able to take breaks throughout so as to not be too exhausted. As scary as it might have been, I felt a sense of relief to be supported by my team and family. Relinquishing control is not something that I am known for, however, having the confidence that others were able to step in and have my back during a time like this speaks volumes. I have shifted from lone-wolfing to being a part of a pack.

The day went smoothly. We had over 100 pleased entrepreneurs. As my mom and friend packed the car, I was reminded of how thankful I was to have their support. Typically, this would have been a very long and exhausting day but because of all their support, I was able to sit back for a bit and allow someone else to take on the "heavy lifting" of the day. It was time for my short drive home. I made a pit stop to pick up dinner and made it home in one piece. I showered and relaxed on the couch for the rest of the evening, feeling full of gratitude and nourishment.

With the pressure of the event behind me, it was time to start thinking about the future of the business. We had a couple more events planned out for the year and the decision to cancel was already on the table. There were so many things going through my mind. I didn't want to feel like a failure because I was unable to host our scheduled events. I also didn't want to feel the pressure of putting together our largest event of the year. For the sake of my health, the right thing to do was to cancel all events for the rest of the year. A final decision was made, now it was time to solidify the call to action. Meanwhile, I had to get a statement written and had to register a team for the annual CIBC Run for the Cure.

It had been a bit over two weeks since my surgery and I was trying to feel some kind of normalcy. I was on short term leave from work, but I felt like there were things that I had left undone. My new focus was to get the house prepped as my mother-in-law was coming from South Carolina to stay with us, so that I could have someone to help me through this journey. It was also a way to help ease my mother's mind as I wouldn't be alone daily.

Let me introduce my mother-in-law to you. She is a spunky lady. Always looking for something new to try, new places to go to or to just experience a plain adventure. She was the exact opposite of my husband who is super quiet and reserved. She was taking a two-day train ride from South Carolina. As a former employee of Amtrak, she absolutely loves the train. My husband tried to convince her to fly, but she insisted on taking the train. She finally arrived after two days with a layover in Grand Central Station at New York City.

As my mother-in-law settled in, a new week was approaching. The week started with my announcement. It was the day the world stood still—at least my world did. I finally posted the statement regarding the Expo cancellation and had a detailed explanation of my "why". Breaking it to the world that I was diagnosed with breast cancer didn't seem like something I wanted to do, but I knew I had to. I owed it to my community to be honest with them so that they had a full understanding of why I had to make the decisions I made regarding the event cancellation. I also thought it important for us women to be honest about the things we experienced, that didn't always get talked about. We were often pillars of strength for our families, friends and colleagues, yet, we didn't shed much light on our own struggles. Personally, I found it difficult accepting help from others. I also found it difficult accepting empathy and compassion. In this moment, I found myself going from being the pillar of strength to being the one who leaned on my community. I could only imagine the many other women who felt the same. I was just not open to receiving and yet I chose being supported by my community over being comfortably perfect.

As the announcement rang out on all my social media channels, my website, and via email, I pretty much held my breath. I stayed clear of my email and didn't check my social media platforms for the day. I avoided answering any phone calls and direct messages. It was a day full of anxiety because I didn't know how to prepare myself for the influx of messages or well-wishes and prayers. Not knowing whether to thank each person individually or how I was even going to put the words together would leave the door open for further conversations and questions. I felt I had been very brave with sharing my truth, but deep diving into my raw emotions about the unfortunate situation or giving a detailed explanation of what I was going through, was going to be too much for me. I was not ready for that level of vulnerability.

I was still avoiding all messages and social media. On a good note, I killed my 6500 Fitbit step goal!!! We decided to go on a day trip to show my mother-in-law Collingwood, Blue Mountain Village, and Wasaga Beach. We strolled around and reminisced about our time at Blue Mountain. We had made some great memories there over the past year. Our stay at the Westin for our anniversary was my first real feeling of relaxation in 2018. I could still smell the coffee I sipped on the balcony every morning while enjoying 24+ degrees Celsius weather. The resort was very quiet at that time and I had a few hours of solace in the morning before everyone else was up. We also told her about the time we spent there as a family at the end of 2018. We had an epic glow in the dark dance party for the kids before an early countdown and rang in the New Year together. Oh, the memories!

We strolled through the village, grabbed lunch at the Firehouse Grill and shopped and admired some art. We got some ice-cream and soaked up the sunny weather that was offered to us and then jumped in the car and headed to Wasaga Beach, the largest freshwater beach in the world.

Understand that my mother-in-law spent most of her life in Miami, and I being Jamaican meant that we were very particular about our beaches. I don't really venture in the water if I can't see the bottom. I know I have a problem, but I just can't shake it. I am used to crystal clear waters, white sand beaches and that added touch of salt! Salt water! I can't swim, so I needed help with floating. We strolled along the boardwalk and admired the hundreds of people gathered on the beach playing games, sun bathing, swimming, building sandcastles, and grilling. It was nice to see how these families were enjoying the last official weekend of the summer despite the fall-like temperatures.

By the end of the day, I was beyond exhausted. I napped in the car on the drive home as this was the most energy I had spent since hosting my event. Even then, I didn't do this much walking so my body was definitely responding. In retrospect, this had been a good few weeks. I had never had this much consecutive free time in my adult life. Of course I would have preferred to experience it due to a different reason, but sometimes we have to give thanks no matter what. August had been a roller coaster, let's see what September would bring.

It's a new month. On any other September, first I would be scrambling to get prepared for our two largest events. The

Immigrant Women's Small Business Expo in Toronto would've been held on the 15th which was exactly two Sundays away. Fortunately for me, this year, I had made the difficult decision to cancel this event. The Ottawa edition was usually held on the last Sunday of September or the first Sunday in October. This year, I postponed this edition due to the lack of availability of our preferred venue. The Ottawa event was a decision that was made earlier in the year, so I was only prepared to take on the Toronto edition. This meant so much to me. It all started with the goal of changing the narrative of immigrant women in Canada. Often, whenever I attended immigrant targeted events, they were job fairs. There was nothing that I could find that catered to immigrant women who wanted to be entrepreneurs. There was that notion that us, as immigrants, were only looked at as the labor class—not as people who could provide jobs to the community.

This year would feel empty without it. If only our participants understood how much it hurt to not go forward with the event this year. I missed the interactions with the guests. I missed hearing the stories of triumph of some of the women who had to overcome many challenges in order to not only get to Canada, but to work hard and become successful entrepreneurs. These guests often thanked me and expressed their appreciation for the work that I did to pull it all together. Little did they know that it is their stories that drive me. The fact that I was able to assemble a group of speakers, sponsors, exhibitors, volunteers, panelists, and guests all in the name of education and inspiration for them, meant so much to me.

I was trying to find ways to fill the void for these next two weeks. I know I was supposed to be focusing on my health, so my void would have to be as close to stress free as possible. There was no better place to start than time with family.

My family had come over to celebrate a bit for the Labor Day long weekend. We were ready to prepare a feast for eight and have fun while doing it. In one room, my middle sister was braiding my hair, while we were talking about the US elections with my mother-in-law. In the other room, my mom and my baby sister were prepping salmon, chicken, veggies, etc. for the barbecue. The kids were downstairs with my husband. The sound of a full house was not something I was used to, but I do enjoy it when it happens. We decided to take a break halfway through my hair and everyone went downstairs as the grilling began. It rained on and off, but overall, the weather was fine. I was thankful it wasn't cold. As my sister focused on finishing all the food prep, we went back and finished my hair, prayed, and ate. We ate and ate and then cleaned and cleaned some more. All in all, the day was great. There were loads of laughter and quality family time. What more could I have asked for to kick off a new month.

Two stimulating days in a row can really do a number on you if you are not recovering from surgery. So can you imagine how I felt? Let me try to paint the picture. I woke up that morning at about 8:30 am and wanted to go back to bed immediately. I slept for another half hour. The only motivation for getting out of bed was the fact that I had a previously scheduled meeting with my Virtual Assistant at 10 am. I rolled out of bed to do the bare minimum of brushing my teeth, washing my face, changing my top, and grabbing some tea. I did have a sleeping win last night. I finally figured out how I could get about half an hour or an hour of sleep on my stomach without squishing my right boob! Getting quality sleep had been so difficult that I had to celebrate the wins.

We ran through our meeting and left with quite a to-do list for the month of September. I might have been battling cancer, but the business could not have been brought to a complete stop. Due to the cancellation of our Expos, I had to find a way to generate additional income for the business. We began working on our business strategy consulting packages early in the summer with a projected launch date of January 2019. Fortunately for us, we already had 90% of the pieces in place, so we decided on a soft launch or a beta version. September was now planned and good to go!

I decided to take it easy for the rest of the day. Couch time and balcony time was the name of the game. I also managed to take a nap for a couple of hours in the evening before we headed out to dinner. Somc days I felt as though I was at 75% and then on days like these, I felt like I was at 50%. "Baby steps," I said to myself.

What a difference a day makes. I woke up with goals that day. I also woke up still feeling exhausted. I made a list of what

I wanted to accomplish today. Laundry, five pages of my book, take my mother-in-law to Zumba and start working on some receipts for my taxes. I managed to do one load of laundry, wrote two pages, and took my mother-in-law to Zumba and that was it.

This day brought a new found appreciation for friends. I managed to reconnect with a friend who I hadn't spoken to in over four years. We spoke for a couple of hours and got caught up on what was going on in our lives. It was in those moments that I could also feel even more reassured with how I handled what most would perceive as a difficult situation. As I shared my story with her, I felt like it was small in comparison to what she was going through. She went through an incident that was very close to costing her everything—her life! What was strange was that her initial reaction to me was that I was going through hell and that her incident wasn't that big of a deal. The perception that most people have about cancer is that they equate it to a death sentence or to the images you see on television of people looking emaciated, pale, and tired due to chemo. Now this is true for some, but it doesn't tell the entire story. I had to remind her that she was close to death and that both our situations were serious in their own rights. It really helped us to put things into perspective. We also vowed to keep in touch and to dedicate more time to self-care.

We understand that there are some things that we cannot control. We could, however, control how we react to certain circumstances that we are placed in during our lives. We could roll with the punches, or we could stress about it. We have to ask ourselves, what would stressing about that situation do? More times than a few, stressing would only make the situation worse. Sometimes in order to decrease our stress level, it helped to recognize what others are going through. Our situation might be minute compared to others. It puts it all in perspective and hopefully does help us remove ourselves from falling down the rabbit hole of stress.

In an effort to break up our days, my mother-in-law and I were trying to find fun activities. We added Zumba to the list as well as weekly visits to the farmers market. This became a weekly tradition because it allowed me to get fresh fruits and vegetables that were essential to my diet, and the walking around kept my body in motion. Who doesn't love starting their day feeling like they have accomplished something that is going toward improving their lives? Our bounty usually included peaches, plums, pears, peas, beans, peppers, tomatoes, zucchini, cucumbers, and asparagus—or whatever they had to offer.

I decided to make the most of my day by not sitting on the couch. It started with me putting a load of blankets in the washing machine and then deciding to sadly dispose of all the flowers that were dead and dying from the many bouquets I had received. The next thing to tackle—my front door. My front door, screen and garage door were coated in dust since the paving construction project on our street. I had wanted to hose them down, but between vacation and surgery, it never got done. I got my hands on the hose, and decided that today was the day to get this done. I was concerned that I would overdo it, but I also didn't want to continue to feel sick. This was the first day that I just wanted to jump into my normal routine. I was tired of feeling like I was in recovery and rest mode. I was tired of being careful. I just wanted an overall feeling of normalcy. To think that before, I would not look forward to doing the day-to-day mundane tasks or chores, but now I am thankful for the ability to do these things, I am both grateful and relieved. I completed the project and felt partially satisfied because I had this new-found motivation to do more.

I decided to take my ambition to the kitchen. I was already feeling exhausted and yet, wanting to feel a little like my old self—the energy filled, ready to take on the world ME!

I blasted some Soca music and let loose to some Lucy by the Queen of Bacchanal-Destra, and decided to wine my way to unpacking all the fruits and vegetables from that week's farmers market trip. Everything was in rhythm, even while doing the dishes, seasoning the lamb for dinner, and cleaning up the kitchen. It was time to slow it down with some reggae while I made my go-to drink of the summer, lemonade. This isn't just any lemonade. It was lavender lemonade made with grilled lemons. I cut the lemons in halves and torched them to give them that grilled flavor. Then I picked some lavender from our garden. The trick to making this lemonade is that once you extract all the juice from the lemons, add honey to it and then the lavender, using hot water to mix them. The lavender flavor will infuse into the lemonade. I had been waiting all summer to take a sip. It was absolutely delicious. By 3:30 pm I was on the couch, feeling exhausted and yet unstoppable. I proceeded to check my emails and went down various rabbit holes online. When I looked up, it was already 5:30 pm and it was time to get back in the kitchen to prepare dinner. This day was the closest to my old normal that I'd had in over a month. I felt like I was hit by a train. I was very tired but happy. It also felt a little like my old self. It was bitter sweet but I made lemonade out of it.

My night ended once again with a phone call from a colleague turned friend. I delivered the news to her earlier that day and was anticipating her call. Some things to note about her was that she was a rule follower, a sweetheart, and someone who did not use foul language. She shocked me at the beginning of our conversation with a Holy F&%K!!! After everything I did to get some normalcy, speaking to her was my highlight of the day. She was one of the few people who I had shared my experience with, who did not doubt how I felt. She listened generously and didn't impart her feelings on the matter. She trusted that if I said I was doing well, then that was so! For that, I was thankful.

You would think that I would sleep in late every morning especially if I kept saying that I woke up tired. I just couldn't help but get out of bed. It was just not in me to sleep in all day. Once again, I had a mission set for the day. Today was all about sheets. Washing all the sheets and blankets in the house. I sat in bed and folded all the laundry from the previous day and then proceeded to put a load in the washing machine. As I looked at the time, I noticed that I had only 30 minutes to shower and get dressed because I had scheduled a lunch date with a colleague.

I had nothing to eat or drink that morning so lunch became brunch, which happened to be my first meal of that day.

Lunch was a breath of fresh air. This particular colleague was like a father-figure. He had always been my favorite person in the office because of his positive and fun spirit toward everything in life. He could always tell when I was not being myself and always took an interest in my well-being. He wanted to catch up with me and to see for himself how I was doing. He was also a source of real life advice because his wife went through the same ordeal about eight years prior and he went through heart surgery some years ago as well.

As we sat and ate, I was able to catch him up on what I had been going through and asked some questions about what to expect. He also told me stories of his recovery and was sure to express how he felt emotionally and physically throughout his process. He also encouraged me to be certain I was 100% before thinking of jumping back into corporate life. He told me not to rush it and to take it easy and heal. I explained to him that the emotional component was still not evident for me, but that physically, I was a mess. I assured him that my goal was to be at 100% before adding any stress to my life. For once, I vowed to put myself first. I had to acknowledge that I wouldn't be any good to anyone, if I wasn't at my peak.

We talked and laughed and took photos to capture the moment. We took a short stroll around the mall after lunch and then found ourselves at Starbucks sipping on beverages and enjoying the scenery. These were the moments I learned to live for—quality down time that was stress free and priceless. Sometimes taking those small moments, even when you are exhausted, can make a big difference.

The other big news for the day was that the NFL season began that day. Football season was like church in our household because my husband is from the football state of Florida. My husband, mother-in-law, and I decided that we would kick this off by going out for wings. At this point I was a zombie because I had no luck in taking a nap in the afternoon despite my efforts. We still managed to get out and enjoy the game. It was hard not to think about the fact that I had my follow up appointment with the surgeon scheduled for the next day. I had a good feeling about it, but lately I had felt the need to try to temper my expectations in order to prepare for the worst.

Today would be the first day since surgery that I saw my surgeon. There was nothing else on my mind throughout the entire day. I stayed in bed as long as I could while being restless—tossing and turning. My appointment was scheduled for 1:45 pm. You would think by then I would have had everything in order, but I don't think I have felt more nervous during this process than I did that day. What drove that feeling was the fact that my entire family was present. What if the news I received was not good? How would I keep it together? That was my greatest fear of the day. It was not the possibility of having to receive the bad news, but about how to ease the blow to everyone while trying to sort out my own feelings.

Fortunately, for me, the news was great. The surgeon informed me that the surgery went very well. He was confident that he got all of the cancer, so technically, I was cancer FREE. He revealed that there was a small amount of cancer cells found in two of the six lymph nodes that were tested. He explained that the amount was miniscule and that he did believe that they acted quickly. My next steps would be to meet with the oncology department for their recommendations. We discussed the possibilities and he assured me that the oncologists would make the best decision based on all the data provided. He did say that perhaps they would take a very aggressive approach due to my age to increase the chances of the cancer never appearing again.

There were a million thoughts going through my head at this point. Obviously, I was very happy to hear the news. In my eyes, I was an A+ patient. I slayed the hell out of cancer. All my bandages were removed, the surgeon admired his handy work and I considered one hurdle behind me. Would I need to do chemo? For how long? How would I feel? What would be the impact on my daily life? How would this affect my family? Would I need to do radiation? How long would I need in order to recover? Would I ever feel 100%? Would I leave all this feeling confident? Most of all, would I make the right decision once presented with my options. I was certain that I would have many more questions, but for now, I was willing to live in the moment and enjoy the good news. Tomorrow was another day.

I had a dose of reality. Would you believe that since the surgery, I had not taken a good look at my breast? I think it would have made it too real. That day was the day I decided to take a look. The doctor removed all of the steri-strips the day before during my post-op appointment. As I looked in the mirror at the scar that was about 5 inches long, my heart sank a bit. It was the first time I really felt the gravity of what I went through. The first time it felt like it wasn't just a little cut that I had stitched up. This made it real.

I felt a wave of emotion come over me. I was not emotional enough to cry and I promised myself that I would not cry over this. It was emotional enough for me to pause and really take the time to reflect on what I really was going through. It also gave me a chance to understand why others around me were being so emotional. They understood the gravity of the situation, but I was just not accepting. It's not that I didn't understand how severe cancer is, it's just that I didn't plan on making this a big deal. I didn't want it to define me. I didn't want it to take up a large part of my life.

We managed to make the day a festive one. After all, we had many things to celebrate. Not only did I get good news from the surgeon, it was also my mother-in-law's birthday. This is the first time she had celebrated her birthday in Canada and it was my first time being able to celebrate with her. We went out and had a wonderful breakfast at her request and ended the day with a delectable dinner at an authentic Cajun restaurant in Toronto. This was the first time since my surgery that I got dressed up, put on make-up, and had a nice evening out. I felt whole again for those few hours. The only difference was that when I got home, I felt like I hadn't slept for days. My energy level was low and was not accustomed to feeling this way.

That week I learned to celebrate the wins. No matter how small and no matter if they seemed like a loss. My prime example was my scar. I could now celebrate my scar because it represented a battle that I had won. I leaped over the first hurdle and I felt as though I could see the finish line.

The celebration spilled over to the next week. I had lunch with a dear friend who I hadn't seen in months. Once again, it gave me a chance to put things in perspective. This was the first time we got a chance to sit and have a conversation since my diagnosis. As I told her everything play-by-play, I started sharing how I felt about the whole thing. I told her how looking at the scar on my breast made me feel. I felt like she was the first person I had a chance to share these feelings with. We have similar personalities, so she understood how I felt about not playing victim and hosting a pity party in this situation. She also knew that I didn't want to dwell on it and that I just wanted to be able to move forward and get back to business as usual.

As we shared stories about the last few months of our lives, we not only shared the bitter, we shared the sweet. We discussed vacations and how we needed them in our busy lives. We discussed family, we discussed business, and we discussed her journey of exhaustion. She shared her journey of realization and of action to get to a better place. It was refreshing to have someone with whom I could share these moments.

As the day came to a close, I had so many things planned. What wasn't planned was an evening of me sleeping on the couch. I had zero energy when I got back from lunch. I wanted to start the week off with a surge. I had solid goals. I did remember from my conversation earlier that I needed to make myself a priority. With that in mind, I decided that taking a nap was a priority. No other chore was necessary to be completed. Tomorrow is another day. If it didn't get done, it would just have to wait. My health and well-being was non-negotiable.

I guess my body really enjoyed that nap because that day, I slept in for an extra hour. It felt odd, but good! I had a lot on my plate and needed to tackle all my paperwork for tax season. I dedicated 3 solid hours of work and felt extremely productive and proud. It was really a good start to the day. The second half of the day brought on more stress than I have had in a while. I took a page out of last week, put everything in perspective, and took a few deep breaths to get myself in the zone. I was looking forward to getting the task complete so that I could get home and do something I hadn't done in a while—go for a walk with a friend. Unfortunately, by the time my errands were completed, I was so exhausted that a walk was off the table. I decided that I would take it easy and have a low-key night.

It was the first Monday Night Football game of the season. I relaxed on the couch and cheered them on. Now I still needed to figure out what the rest of my week would look like.

Eventually, it was my first day back at work. Although, not on a full time basis, I was cleared to work from home for a maximum of 5 hours per day. I must be honest about how I felt about this. One part of me was sad, sad to have to add another level of stress to my day. I was also sad to think that my full day of rest, without thinking about the corporate hustle, was over. However, I was happy to jump in and catch up on what I was missing. I wanted to see how my team was doing and to still feel like a valued contributor to my department.

I turned on my computer for the first time since being back from my short leave. It took about 5 minutes for it to start-up and about 20 minutes for Outlook to load all my emails. When all was said and done, I had a little over 1000 emails to sort through. I was in no rush to go through these. I gave myself one week to go through all the emails. The first day was full of excitement as it was energizing to get back into the game. I managed to go through a few hundred emails before calling it quits. Besides, I still had to take care of some other items on my to-do list and ensure that I took time to relax.

So, how was I feeling physically? I was still exhausted. I tried to make it through the day without napping, but it was difficult. Some of my burnout might have been caused by not sleeping well. I was still unable to sleep comfortably on my right side or on my stomach. I was fearful that this would become the new normal. I still did have some hope that I would sleep easy again, sooner rather than later.

Day 2 of my return to the corporate world—I spent another 4 hours sifting through emails and felt like progress was being made. Day 2 felt hopeful. There was one exception, which seemed to be a constant. My energy level continued to be low. I also couldn't fall asleep the previous night. In my waking moments, I read through a few articles to try to prepare for my pending appointment with the medical oncologist, with one week and one day to research as much as necessary and to formulate all my questions. I was also concerned about how I would function during the treatment. I like being prepared. I was also optimistic that I would only have to deal with radiation and that chemo was not on the table. Reading all the articles about how radiation works and what to expect was very helpful. Preparation was key for my mental stability. Venturing into unknown territories was very uncomfortable for me.

On another note, there had been some new sensations in the incision areas of my breast and arm. I had begun to feel sudden shooting pains. On a scale from one to ten, it started at about five or six, increasing in frequency. If this was a sign of healing, I was ready to take it in stride.

This brought me back to a conversation I had with a nurse a couple of weeks ago. She was the nurse who removed the staples from the incision under my right arm. When she saw the scar on my breast while dressing it, she mentioned the cut was right across the nerves. It made absolute sense to me as there was no real sensation when I ran my finger along the wound. This was different when removing the staples from under my arm as it was an ordeal. The first few came out smoothly with just a pinch of pain. The final staple, however, was twisted and it took about 5 minutes for it to be pulled out. I had to clench my jaw and scream internally throughout this process. I had thoughts of what it would be like to just leave it there. I felt as if my flesh was being ripped in order to remove the staple and what was keeping me motivated in this moment of endurance, was the nurse's constant words of compassion. I wanted to forget that physical trauma I experienced that day.

While the pain was rolling in, so were my friends. I had a pleasant visit from a long-time friend from university. It was nice to catch up even if it was for a small amount of time. We reminisced about our days at the University of Windsor and filled each other in, on what our family members were up to. We hadn't seen each other in about fifteen years, so you can imagine how much there was to talk about. The unfortunate part about all this was that it took a life changing situation for us to reconnect. I wish this wasn't the case, however, I am a believer in what is to be, will be. It was meant for us to reconnect even if it was due to an unfortunate situation so I promised myself to keep in touch from then on. I was certain that it would not take another fifteen years or another life altering moment to connect.

The world didn't stop for me. People were still getting married and babies were still being born. That day, I had the pleasure of attending my first gender reveal party. It was a long drive to get there but it was worth it. Celebrating life really helps to put things into perspective. Every day is important. Not just birthdays. Every single day. It was the farthest I had driven on my own since the surgery. It was exhilarating to be celebrating with friends again. I was very mindful of how long I stayed because my energy level was fluctuating and I needed to be alert for my long drive home. I was happy that I was able to spend some quality time with friends before heading out for my drive home to rest.

Time flew by. It was time for my mother-in-law to head home for a couple of weeks before she came back to Canada. We decided that it would be best for her to return because if it was determined that I would have to do chemo, she would be there for my daily support. I wasn't sure how my body would react to chemotherapy. We were hoping that I did not have to take this route, but also prepared for it if it was necessary. It was all in the hands of science and the medical oncologist.

Week two of working from home—It dawned on me that I needed to have some kind of structure to my day. Oftentimes, we work so hard and we get accustomed to the fast hustle of life, so structuring the day would allow things to fall into place, because there was always plenty to do. Typically on those days, we dream of having time off to relax. Now that I had been blessed—yes, I said blessed—with this time off, I was now grasping for structure. I had more than enough on my plate for the business that needed completion. I also now had the time to work on items that were put on the back burner. There was no shortage of tasks to complete, and I craved the daily structure of having to wake up at a certain time, drive into the office, work the allotted hours, return home, and then work on the business. It was strange, I know. I needed to pivot and learn to create a schedule that included daily relaxation and time for work. I needed to take a look at what my new normal would look like and start working toward it.

I decided to try to set out a schedule for the day. It was not perfect, but it was only day 1. I chose to review all the documents that I had received so far from my surgeon. What exactly was my diagnosis? According to the initial reports of the two biopsies performed, it was invasive ductal carcinoma, Nottingham grade III and metastatic carcinoma. What exactly did all that jargon mean?

The Nottingham grade comes from a scale that measures the normalcy of the cells being analyzed. The cells are measured based on their normalcy and how fast they are dividing.

Carcinoma is a term used to describe any cancer in the thin lining of an organ. In this case, it was my breast. These cells developed in the ducts of the breast and because the report indicated they were invasive, they had the ability to metastasize, or simply said, they had spread to other areas of the body.

The second set of biopsy was performed from samples taken from my body during surgery. The surgeon not only removed the tumor which was 2.3 centimeters, but he also removed 6 nodes from my right armpit. Humans have an average of 30 nodes under their arms. The number varies from person to person on a very wide range. Both the tumor and the nodes were biopsied and the results were invasive. What the hell does that mean?

Yes, I thought the same thing when I looked at the report. I'm no microbiologist and I am definitely not an oncologist, so I will leave the scientific details right here. The other important piece of information about my type of cancer was that it wasn't aggressive, however, it was estrogen positive. There was a lot of information to decipher and comprehend, and it took for me to experience cancer to become cancer-educated. It was very important for me to know as much as possible before my appointment so that I could understand the reason behind the treatment chosen by my doctor. I was certain my appointment with the medical oncologist would be one full of new information.

My lovely mother, Susan and I circa 1981 in Jamaica. My little pigtails were definitely a fashion statement. Let the record show that socks and sandals were in style then too!

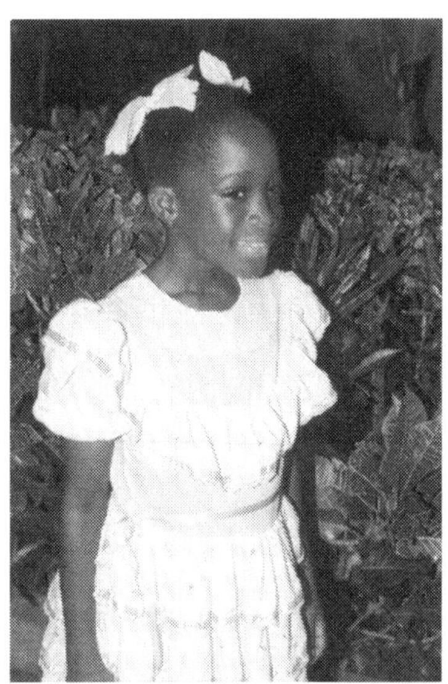

My 8th birthday outfit. Ribbons and pigtails were clearly my style.

My 8th and 9th birthday cakes were my most memorable cakes. It had a solid sugar basket set within one cake and the other was a barbie. These were also the first "birthnight" parties that I could remember.

My very first buzz cut in order to get ahead of the hair loss. I felt free!

Wig shopping was something I never saw in my future. This was my favorite of the bunch. I still have it stored away in a box. It might make an appearance on a bad hair day.

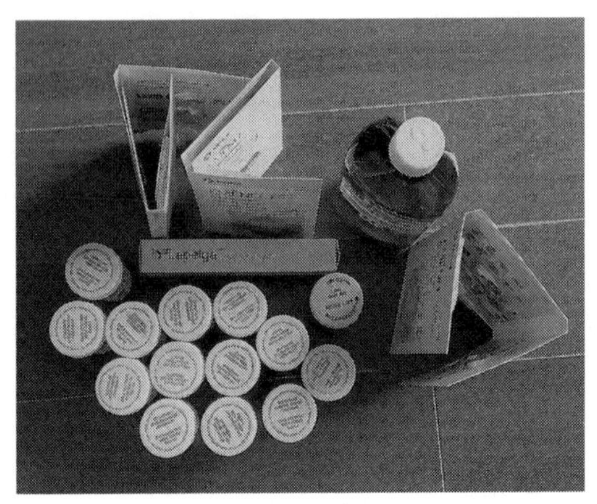

My drug cocktail for each round of chemo.

My outfit for our first CIBC Run for the Cure in Toronto. Our team name is October's Finest Boobs.

Our very first group for the Toronto edition of the CIBC Run for the Cure. This was two weeks before my first round of chemo. I am so thankful to everyone who walked, cheered and donated that day.

The pandemic forced us to be more creative with our celebrations. I finished my final treatment in April 2020 and social distancing was necessary. This was my family's celebration for me! Shown here are my sister Doujoné and my nephew Darius. My mother and husband were in the background and my other sister Ginel and nephew Jacob were on the phone. What a surprise that was!

My 40th birthday celebration filled my heart. My sisters and I definitely had a blast

My wonderful husband and I putting on a brave face and having fun in Madrid, Spain right before I had to get my lumpectomy

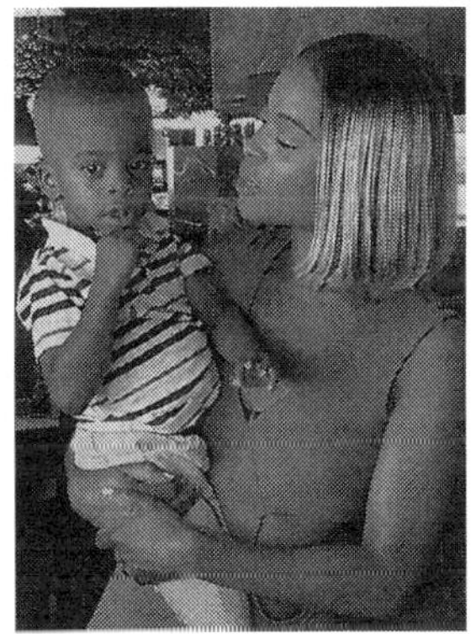

Familyover everything!

Me, post treatment and post COVID-19 back doing what I love to do. I am seen here at our Amplify Your Voice Conference.

6

CHEMOTHERAPY

Can we say hooray!!! It is my last day of radiation and I don't have enough words to describe how I feel. Friday was a holiday (Good Friday) and would have originally been my final day of treatment if it were a regular day. As luck and fate would have it, an opening was available for the first thing Saturday morning. As I got into my car, and drove to the hospital, I smiled at the sun and felt a sense of peace. Everything seemed brighter to me. I tried to be conscious of everything—I was engrossed in the quietude of the world around me as I took the drive. I arrived to the calming emptiness of the parking lot and later to the welcoming cheerfulness of the volunteers at the hospital check-in. The sun was shining ever so brightly, filtering through the slats of the radiation wing. The peacefulness of my surroundings as I walked into the room and lay on the machine bed for one last time comforted me. All is well.

"Don't worry, about a thing. Cause every little thing, is gonna be alright."

I developed a habit of singing throughout the few minutes of the treatment for all 30 sessions. This time, I was singing the same song I sang when I went into surgery—Three Little Birds by Bob Marley. I felt happy. I felt thankful. I felt forever grateful.

Radiation was its own kind of acrobatics—at least this time, I was laying down. My couture was my hospital gown. As I sashayed down my personal runway to the radiation room for the past twenty-nine days, I had enough practice with my runway walk to be Naomi Campbell on my last stride. Laying on the radiation bed, striking various poses, holding my breath, finding my angles, as the laser beams found their tattooed targets on my body, it was the finishing touch to the second phase of this show.

As I left, the radiation technicians said goodbye and wished me well. Walking toward my car in the parking lot, my phone rang. It was my mother. Perfect timing! We talked about the sense of relief we both felt that the treatment was over. The pandemic was looming over us, it was nice to know that I did not have any commitments outside the house. I could only imagine the worry she had been feeling every day since I told her about my diagnosis coupled with the possibility of being exposed to the virus. I sensed her partial sense of relief. As I neared being home, I started planning the long walk I would take. I wanted to clear my head and enjoy the lovely weather on tap. I turned onto my street, turned into my complex and drove toward my house. I was greeted with the best surprise a girl could dream of.

As I drove toward my driveway, I saw balloons and cars with signs in what could be the only form of celebration that was fitting for the superstar that I had become. My family refused to allow this accomplishment to go by without acknowledgment. I was overwhelmed with emotion. Along with my sense of relief, I now felt a sense of joy and immense love. To see the faces of my husband, mother, sisters, and my nephews, to know they shared my joy in my completion of treatment. We could all finally start looking forward to my healing and a new chapter in my life.

As I bid my celebration committee farewell, I decided it was time to take that walk I had been dreaming of. It is fitting that on Easter weekend; I am facing my very own resurrection. I laced up my sneakers, put on my headphones, turned on my best liked podcast—My Favorite Murder—and set out to enjoy the sunshine. It's only fitting that True Crime is my genre—I just killed cancer! As I strolled, I took the time to reflect on all that I had been through over the past 11 months. This had been beyond my wildest dreams. My body had been put through more than I thought I could handle, but I felt like my life had prepared me for this—I felt a sense of relief and pride, a sense of hope for what was in store for the rest of my life.

I also took some time to reflect. To reflect on all the things I took for granted. Going through treatment made me miss the simplest things, like the taste of the food I ate, being able to work out, to soak up the sun on a patio with friends, to sleep with ease, to enjoy a glass of water, and to move with flow. I especially missed taking walks like these. I loved going for walks and taking that time for myself to reflect and to listen to podcasts.

Enough of reflecting ... I was ready to move forward and most of all ready for a vacation. My last vacation was one for the books, but there was also a lot on my mind then. I couldn't wait to do it all over again.

Earlier, I was overwhelmed with information! Truly overwhelmed. I felt more emotional than I had felt throughout this entire ordeal. I was at a loss for words. I was confused, sad, and lost.

Before I met him, the first appointment with the medical oncologist, required me to get a badge created to use each time I visited the hospital. I familiarized myself with the self-check-in kiosk and gathered some additional new patient information as I was new to the oncology wing. I was told that I should wear that badge whenever I went there. I felt like an employee!

I was ushered into a room by one of the lovely nurses at Credit Valley Hospital. Did I mention that everyone there was a breath of fresh air? They really are. She went through a very long questionnaire with me that I filled out in the waiting room. This questionnaire was six pages and it covered everything from pain level, to emotions, to support. It was thorough. I was both impressed and apprehensive. It really made me feel vulnerable, but despite all that, I answered honestly.

The medical oncologist entered the room and I do not remember much of that conversation before he said the dreaded word—chemo. The word I did not want to hear was now in my face. His recommendation for six cycles, followed by radiation, followed by five years of hormone therapy, seemed overwhelming. My mind went blank. I recall seeing his lips moving and hearing a voice, but not quite comprehending what he was saying. Nothing he said was registering for me. Fortunately, my husband was there with me and everything that was being said, was also being given to me as a part of my reading material. It was a lot of information to process.

Not only did he give me all that information, I was offered an alternative treatment option. He wanted to get me to be a part of a clinical trial. The only thing was, the trial was set up for women over forty. I was six weeks away from my 40th birthday so I didn't see a problem with getting on the trial list. He had to consult with the ones in charge of the trial to get special permission for me to be included in the study. The great part of this study was that it gave me a small possibility of not having to do chemo based on preliminary test results. So ended appointment number one.

I got to use my fancy hospital badge at my next pit stop. I had to do blood work before my appointment. Apparently, this would be my new normal as I would be required to do blood work prior to each chemo cycle—if chemo was the route being taken. I flashed my fancy badge with authority and went off to fill some vials of blood.

My final stop of the hospital train that day was with radiology. That stop was quick and easy. An introduction to the doctor and a quick overview of how radiology works was all there was to it. She informed me that we would have a more in-depth conversation once I was nearing the end of chemotherapy.

I needed to clear my head. It was still going in circles since the previous day. I laid out all the paperwork I received and went through them all. There was so much I didn't think of. I had to consider losing hair, eyebrows, and even eyelashes. Not being able to drink or eat citrus food. Staying away from the sun. That was punishment for this island girl because the sun makes me happy. There would be changes in my skin. Low platelet count, low white blood cell count, mouth sores, tingling fingers and toes, possible swelling, diarrhea, eye problems, and more! Granted, I might get lucky and not all these things would apply to me, but I did not know which way the pendulum would swing. The most common thing we always associate with chemotherapy is hair thinning or hair loss. This journey had opened my eyes to many details about cancer that I was so oblivious to.

After going through all the paperwork, I plotted all my upcoming appointments on my desk calendar. I also took the time to record things I would have liked to do for fun, just so there was a balance and that I would feel like there is some normalcy in my life. Once everything was captured, I felt a bit of ease and miraculously, my head stopped hurting. I was back to feeling more like my old self.

The day was getting started as I had an optometrist appointment scheduled as directed by my oncologist. Did you know that chemotherapy could affect your eyesight as well? I headed downtown, and was excited about my appointment because the optometrist is a dear friend and this would give us a chance to catch up over lunch. I got to support a female owned business, picked out some new frames, and got my old lady eyes checked. While our Thai lunch date was nourishing for my belly, catching up with a friend also nourished my soul.

Up next was a movie date with another friend. This was the first time in a very long time that I was double booked for the day. Certainly, the first time since surgery that I could remember. It was going to be a late night. The movie was average, but we still had a blast. We went out for dinner, it was an appetizer for me because I was still full from lunch, and then we talked for 4 hours in the theater parking lot, after the movie was done. Gotta love those summer nights!

I was tired. Very tired. Being out all day and getting in after 1 am is not the same when you are in recovery mode. I managed to sleep in until about 10 am the next day, and I was still tired. I had lunch plans with some of my team members from work, and there was no way I was going to cancel because as much as I enjoyed my time off work, I did miss them. We met at one of my favorite places to eat on a weekend—or weekday at that. If you have never been to Joey's, then you are missing out. I felt a sense of apprcciation and love from my team. I made it a point to treat them with respect and to always let them know that I was there for them. They too let mc know how much they were there for me and how much they were praying that I would have a speedy recovery. It was my turn to receive. After a few hours of catching up, it was time to head home to rest as I was still tired from the night before.

It was a new week and it was going to be interesting, to say the least. I needed to organize all the paperwork that I had received since my first mammogram, review all the information to ensure that I wasn't missing anything, and start going into the office on a reduced schedule. The past few weeks of working from home were very relaxing. It would be refreshing to reintroduce some structure in my day. I was also apprehensive about it. I hoped my body was ready for this step. I planned on taking it step by step as my health is paramount.

Another day and yet another appointment and this one was definitely another emotional one. Not enough for me to cry, but enough for me to have that tight feeling in my chest and that light headedness that happens when you feel anxiety. This wasn't a positive rush. I had an appointment as suggested by my medical oncologist with a reproductive specialist. I was very apprehensive about taking this appointment, but I agreed because I fully understood his stance. I was thirty-nine, married, and with no children, therefore, he wanted us to speak to someone in the fertility field to discuss all my options. Based on the treatment plan that was given to me on my previous appointment, my hormones would be out of whack until I was at least forty-five. This coupled with the fact that my cancer type was estrogen positive meant that they would more than likely force my body into early menopause.

The appointment was another interesting one. After going through a seven-page-long questionnaire inquiring about everything from surgical history to sexual history and much more, I finally went in for my assessment. While sitting in the waiting room and watching the constant flow of people in and out of the office, a few things dawned on me. I started to recall the many fertility clinics I had seen while driving around the Greater Toronto Area. I also started recalling the many people I knew who had struggled with fertility or who had undergone hysterectomies. I started to wonder if waiting this long to have children and focusing on my career instead was the right thing to do. Immediately I started second guessing myself and feeling incredibly emotional.

I am a woman who believes that everything happens for a reason. Sometimes, we cannot see or even begin to understand the reasons we go through certain experiences in life. We try to justify when our journeys take us down some terrible roads. With all these things on my mind, whatever I was experiencing, I trust that it was for a particular reason. There is no testimony without a test, and I have always vowed to make my entire life one full of testimonies.

My appointment wasn't without some kind of question mark, but I cherished the moments of honesty shared between the doctor and me. She was very understanding of my situation and displayed a level of empathy that I couldn't have imagined. She reviewed all possible options and discussed the likelihood of success for each. When the dust settled, and all the data was discussed, I fully understood what I stood to lose—the possibility of having children. I would like to say I was surprised, but I was more crushed because I felt like my body was broken. I left the office feeling even more overwhelmed than I did the week before, but with a promise to focus on staying positive and conquering cancer. I could only climb one mountain at a time and this one was like Everest.

As much as I would like to think this was not affecting me, I knew I was an emotional wreck. I needed to find a support system. After speaking with my husband and a couple of friends, I was able to feel a little bit less stressed, but not enough where I could move on and focus on my pending treatment.

The day wasn't all about being emotionally drained and getting bad news. I heard back from the trial doctors at the hospital and was approved to be a part of the clinical trial. That was the news that was needed to give me more hope and to solidify the fact that I had to move forward and shift my focus back to where it should be—on my recovery and the fact that I planned on going into the office the next day, for the first time since my surgery.

First-day-of-work nerves—I didn't think I would feel this nervous to return to work after only being off for a couple of months. I wasn't nervous about the responsibilities; I was nervous about dealing with the reactions and emotions of my colleagues. Being the center of attention was not my cup of tea. I could handle attention and handle it very well, I just preferred to not be put in that position. It was a very warm welcome. Everyone was very happy to see me, but they didn't ask too many questions—which I was very happy about. My team brought me flowers and made me feel that much more special.

Day 2 of being in the office and it was starting to feel like I was back on track. There was so much to catch up on and so little time to get it done. I had also been focused on trying to build our walk team for the upcoming CIBC Run for The Cure (TM) in support of breast cancer. I was so excited to have 25 walkers on our team! It was humbling to know that all these people were willing to walk to support me, but before we could even consider the walk, there was a lot to prepare. There was also the pending thought of the possibility of chemotherapy.

"You might feel like you've peed yourself." That was my take-home message of the day. It was the day I experienced my first CT Scan. What an interesting experience that was. I feel like I keep saying that all the experiences thus far were interesting, but I choose to live in the moment and soak up as much information as possible. I also recognize that everyone's experience is different and that not everyone can suppress the thought of being in a hospital and being poked and prodded all the time. We can call it a superpower for now.

Back to the CT scan. I made sure I ate a very large lunch as they required me to not eat 2 hours prior to the appointment. I arrived at the hospital and they put an IV port in my arm. I had to drink the equivalent of four to five cups of a fluid and allow enough time to pass for it to work its way through my body. After about an hour or so, I was called in. If you have never seen a CT machine, it looks like something straight out of a time travel movie. I laid on the platform, the nurse attached the IV to my port and the platform moved through the ring that was standing at 90 degrees to the ground. It was as if I was hovering back and forth through a portal. I did mention I had a superpower, right? The machine told me when to hold my breath and when to breathe freely.

The pee comment? This is where it came into play. An iodine based fluid was fed through my IV. It gave me a warm sensation from head to toe. It particularly felt warm in the crotch area and gave me the sensation of peeing myself. Fortunately for all of us, there were no accidents. The scan took about 4 minutes to complete followed by a 10-minute wait before the port was removed. This was just another day at the hospital amongst my superhero friends.

Juggling these appointments and preparing for a breast cancer walk felt therapeutic. In one breath, I was taking the steps to take care of myself and my health, and in the other, I was doing my part to raise funds for research, and to bring awareness to help others who might have been afflicted with this disease. A friend and I made our way to the office of the Canadian Cancer Society to pick up the team shirts, and as we walked in, I felt a sense of pride. On the wall was their mission statement painted in oversized letters. I was proud to be doing my part to assist in the journey of improving the life of those with cancer and to donate to the mission of eradicating the disease.

Having such an inspiring day to break up the pending task list was a relief. I had to get back to reality. I had yet another day of information overload ahead of me. The morning was typical, as I woke up, I had breakfast and took some time to catch up with a friend. I was anxious about the pending chemotherapy information session. I was thankful that the group was small with only about 12 people present. We endured a 3-hour talk delivered by an oncology nurse, a pharmacist, a nutritionist, and a Social Worker. The presentation was thorough and recapped some of the details previously received, but also included a lot of new ones. There were so many things to consider while going through chemotherapy. This was very necessary. I cannot speak to the protocol at other hospitals, but the team at Credit Valley was very thorough. There was no lack of information.

They provided us with a booklet that detailed everything to expect. There was also information about who to contact for additional support. They detailed external services that could be used for everything from wigs to physical activity support and emotional support groups. I learned that there were foods that were off limits during chemo. Who knew? The most disappointing was alcohol. To be honest, I knew that I would lose some of my loves, but I also understood that it was only for a short time. We talked about the precautions that had to be taken during treatment with family and friends. I would have to stay out of the sun as well. Fortunately for me, if I did have to go ahead with chemotherapy, the treatment would be primarily during the winter months. I wouldn't miss being outside then. I do not have an affinity for cold weather. I am being polite, quite frankly, I loathe the cold. As an island girl, made from sun and sand, the cold could never be my home.

Armed with another pile of documents, I spent the next couple of days reviewing everything. I wanted to ensure that I had all my questions answered and if not, had new questions for the oncology team. For me, this entire process was an experience. Staying informed was also one way of me staying calm. I like to have time to analyze processes before moving forward. If I could understand the possibilities, then I could focus on keeping my stress level low, which would help my body in the long run with the healing process.

It was an early start to a day full of motivation. The annual CIBC Run for the Cure (™) across Canada was magical. My day started at about 6:30 am. Too early if you ask me. We had to meet at our spot at 8:30 am, so there was no work around getting up early. I woke up and donned my pink or should I say coral outfit and was ready to rock. The weather forecast was a bit troublesome as it was predicting rain for the morning. We brought along a few ponchos and willed the rain to go away. To our surprise, the rain stopped as soon as we parked the car at our meeting spot.

We met with our group, donned our team shirts, screaming "October's Finest Boobs" in bright pink on the back of our shirts, and we headed to the start area. Walking in was an attack on our senses. There was so much going on. Music playing, food stations, registrations, teams dressed in costumes, photo stations, and more! We soaked it all in and took some group photos to capture the moments. We participated in the warm up and took off to the start line. I was in awe as I saw the sea of people walking. It went on and on like a never ending sea of pink. We heard that there were close to 10,000 people who participated, but to see them in reality was heart-warming. All these people were touched by breast cancer and they all came out to support a worthy cause. It still brings me back to knowing that every person who I have had a conversation with, about my journey, either had battled breast cancer or had one or two people directly related to them who have been through it.

As we all walked, we broke off into smaller groups and went at our own pace. We talked and laughed and admired outfits of other participants. The 5K went by quickly. As we got to the finish line, the music was pumping and the energy was invigorating. We high fived, took photos, had some snacks, and started exploring. We all laughed and talked for about an hour before we dispersed and carried on with the rest of our day.

After the physical and sensory exertion of the day, a nap was necessary. The pain in my legs also reminded me that I had not done anything that resembled exercise in months! It also reminded me that I should push myself to be a bit more active because it would be better for my physical health and healing. I decided to take it easy for the rest of the day and lounged on the couch, watched football, and made a batch of hot sauce to break up my evening.

The magic of the day would be all the motivation I needed to help me make it through this journey.

The next day I was still on a "high" from the walk. Looking back at all the photos and videos on my timeline and on my phone brought me joy and hope. Recalling some of the conversations I had with total strangers and the messages of motivation warmed my heart. I was truly inspired and thankful.

My mother-in-law was back in town the very next day, so that we had more hands on deck to help as the start of my chemo regimen neared. I had two days' worth of appointments within that week and the next day, I would find out for certain, if chemo was a go.

It was another emotionally heavy day. It was the moment when everything got real. I spent some more quality time at the hospital meeting with both the oncologist and a nurse. The oncologist revealed the results for the oncotype test that was sent out earlier. My score was 30, which was above the magic number of 18 that we hoped for. With a score above 18, it confirmed that chemotherapy was essential. We were hoping for a way to avoid it all together and jump straight to radiation, but there was no such luck. We reviewed my chemotherapy plan and further explained what I should expect. They confirmed the type of chemo that I would be administered. Yes. There are different types because there are different cocktails of drugs. My chemo was a promise that I would definitely lose my hair. Not maybe, not probably, but surely. My nurse reviewed all the emergency phone numbers to call, and the many possible scenarios for using them. They handed me my prescription and went through in detail what each medication was meant for. She explained that the pharmacist would review it with me again and that everything would be clearly identified for ease of use.

I gathered my new stack of paperwork and made my way to the hospital pharmacy.

After waiting for about an hour and a half, the pharmacist called me in to explain when and how to use my medication. To my surprise, she had seven items. Yes, seven! All these were to be used just for the first round of chemotherapy and there were five more rounds to go. There was also a bottle of mouthwash that contained lidocaine to help if I got mouth sores. There were tons of medications and it was overwhelming. All I kept thinking was that if I was not feeling like myself for days after the treatment, how in the world would I remember the permutations and combinations of these medications and what if I totally screwed them up? The pharmacist reassured me that they would provide me with a chart that outlines my medication schedule on day 1 of chemo. If not, my plan was to color code the bottles and set color reminders in my phone so that I didn't have to think about it.

I left the hospital, ran an errand and decided to decompress on the couch. It was a lot to unpack, especially that the first day of chemo was one week away. My oncologist and I were strategic when we chose the chemotherapy dates. There was a lot to consider as there was a specific window, post-surgery, where chemo should begin for best results. Personally, I was focused on my birthday. I was turning the big 4-0!!! It looked like it was gearing up to be the most low-key birthday that I could remember. The irony of it all is that I was about to start chemotherapy on my birthday month as well as in the month that is dedicated to raise awareness to the disease I was trying to overcome. Cheers to my rebirth!

Another day brought me to my new favorite place—Credit Valley Hospital. Why do most tests at the hospital involve drinking copious amounts of water? The logical part of me understands why, but it doesn't make it any easier. I was off to my bone density test. What did this involve? I arrived at the hospital at 7:45 am and got a radioactive dye injected into my arm. Fifteen minutes later, I was told that I had to drink about eight cups of water over the period of 3 hours before returning for my scan. That meant I had 3 hours to spend. What a luxury. Especially when I think of how busy my life was.

In 3 hours, my mother-in-law and I shopped for our Canadian Thanksgiving items as well as purchased a card for my wedding anniversary. We had a lot to be grateful for in October. We made it back to the hospital after I drank the required amount of water. Needless to say, I needed to find a bathroom! The scanning process lasted about 2 hours and I left the room thrice to use the bathroom! This was the final test before I had to move on to the next stage.

We headed home to have a low key celebration for our wedding anniversary. My mother-in-law decided to treat us by baking her famous whipping cream pound cake. While she did her magic in the kitchen, my husband and I grabbed Japanese food, packed the car with snacks, and headed to the drive-in to watch Joker. One constant for us when celebrating our anniversary is Japanese food. There is always sushi or something else and relaxation. This tradition fell into our laps as we happened to visit a local Japanese restaurant that has since burned down for our very first wedding anniversary. The experience was exactly what we were looking for—relaxing. We try to avoid going out to fancy meals for this occasion. We relax and do something that we love doing with each other. Once the movie ended, we headed home in time to have cake with my mother-in-law and recapped the day's adventure.

After having a few hectic days in a row, I looked forward to some simplicity and a set schedule. It was business as usual as I went back to my new normal of rolling out of bed at about 9 am. I sipped my morning coffee, checked emails, and made a couple of phone calls before I headed into the office. A 4-hour work day was literally what the doctor ordered. It was just enough to not put me over the edge, but also left me that feeling of productivity and accomplishment. I picked up dinner for my mother-in-law and me, and we settled in and watched Thursday Night Football.

The following day started with a breakfast date that was three years in the making. Have you ever met someone and instantly clicked? That was how it happened with this fiery redhead. We met doing business and knew we would become fast friends. She was bubbly and full of life and was exactly what I needed at that moment. We laughed and talked about our business challenges, business successes, and just about life and made a promise to ourselves to not allow too much time to pass before catching up again. It was also a good chance to speak with yet another person who had a close family member affected by cancer. She shared details of what it was like to see her family member go through chemo as well as some of the side effects that they experienced. My biggest concern was not knowing how my body would react to chemo. A part of me could not wait to have my first round so that I knew what to expect going forward. Fortunately, I didn't have to wait that long to find out.

Next stop was the office. It was my second to last day and I just wanted to get things wrapped up. I was still a bit worried about how things would progress in my absence, but I also needed to focus on getting well. I pushed myself and got as much done as one could, in 4 hours, and moved along to my next stop for the day—Downton Abbey!

I can't believe it had been two weeks since the movie Downton Abbey was released and I had not yet seen it. I still missed watching the television series on a weekly basis. The movie was more than I could have expected. The company was great too. It was a perfect ending to a long day.

The day before a Thanksgiving feast can be hectic, but we made the best of it. It all started with a trip to St. Jacob's Market. I hadn't been to that market in years! I recalled that it unfortunately burned down a few years ago and had to be rebuilt, so it was exciting to be able to take a drive and experience the new and improved market. It didn't disappoint us! The market was jam-packed but also full of so many goodies. We shopped for all the items on our list for Thanksgiving and browsed around to find more goodies. We bought shea butter, flowers, many fruits, and vegetables and decided to take our shot at the long line up for their famous apple fritters. We were in line for about 30 minutes and it was worth the wait. We bought our dozen fritters to go and one each to eat right away. It was piping hot and delicious. We headed back to Mississauga to stop at the supermarket to purchase the additional items on our list for the next day's dinner. We shopped and prepped for the masses that would be descending upon us.

Happy Thanksgiving! I love holiday celebrations. It is a great way to have family and friends over to enjoy each other's company. We had a perfect mix of family, old friends, and new ones. It was also my mother-in-law's first Thanksgiving in Canada since our wedding nine years ago. So this was a special-edition Thanksgiving for our family. It was an early start to the day. I was up by 9 am and started cooking 2 hours later. What was on the menu? Everything. There was smoked turkey, curry chicken, grilled salmon, macaroni and cheese, rice and peas, cornbread stuffing, grilled veggies, steamed cabbage, cranberry sauce, fried plantain, cucumber and tomato salad, kale salad and loads of baked goods.

At about 5 pm it was time to eat, drink, and be merry. It was about fifteen of us and we had a blast. I ate until I couldn't move. It was an enjoyable yet uncomfortable feeling—that perfect Thanksgiving feeling. As we all chatted and joked about our lives, I felt thankful to be able to host our family and friends for yet another year. As everyone started departing, we cleaned up and relaxed. As the night went on, I started to think about my week ahead. T minus 3 days until I start my first treatment. My level of anxiety was probably at 30 percent.

I took advantage of the early voting polls as it was Thanksgiving holiday. It was impressive to see how many people were taking advantage of early voting. As I walked away from the poll, I felt a sense of pride. Exercising the right to vote was an honor. I felt like I was making proud those who fought to give me this right. I took my voting rights very seriously. I spent the rest of the day on the couch relaxing because through my experiences, I have learned that rest is important in the rejuvenation process. I had one more day of work remaining for the year and I needed to get into the mindset of completion. I needed to feel like I had crossed everything off my list and that all would be well in my absence. I was practicing the art of letting go. It was T minus 2 days until my first treatment.

It was my last day of work for about 10 months! It was bitter sweet. I was thankful to be able to have the time off to focus on my health and well-being. I was also thankful to work for a company that was so supportive and compassionate. I wrapped up a few items and said my goodbyes.

On the home front, it was a relaxing evening. There was nothing to concern myself with. I was now focused on what the next day would look like.

It was the day—October 16th, 2019. I made my way to the hospital with my mother and my mother-in-law. My appointment was for 10:45 am. I had to take my first tablet an hour before that. We arrived at the hospital at about 10:30 am and checked-in. They called me into the chemo lounge and the process began.

The lounge was a new experience. I was able to choose my chair from the ones that were not being used. Each station had a super comfy lounge chair, a TV, and a coat closet. It was cozy. It also had enough room for me to invite a couple of guests. They had me seated in a comfortable lounge chair and set me up on an IV. Before the IV started, I had to take five tablets. Did I mention that I absolutely hate taking pills no matter the size? It has been a lifelong problem of mine. Nevertheless, I took all five of them, but not without being dramatic. I frowned, I grimaced, I cried, I rolled my eyes. I even gave the nurses permission to laugh at me because I knew I was being a drama queen.

As the session started, I felt my entire body get cold as the solution traveled up my arm. The nurses discussed the option of having a port which is a device inserted beneath the skin that makes it easier to administer treatment or draw blood. The port would be in place for the entirety of the treatment process. I was thankful that the veins in my hands were strong enough to handle the ever so large needle that was used for the intravenous process. I was supplied with a warm blanket, reclined the chair, and watched the time go by as my very first chemo treatment was underway. Another side effect to note was that I started to have a metallic taste in my mouth once the treatment started. My senses were heightened as I wanted to take note of all my side effects.

As we sat there for 2.5 hours, we laughed and chatted about everything imaginable. We had a pharmacist come in and speak with us for about half an hour about each of the medications, the side effects of chemo, and gave me a schedule for taking more pills over the next four days. During the administering of the medication, I found out I was the newbie on the block. All other patients in my chemo lounge had been through this for many cycles. I got some sound advice from one of the other patients about oral health. To avoid any mouth sores, she advised me to gargle and rinse my mouth with baking soda, salt, and warm water mix. She suggested that I should start using it before any signs of sores and use it frequently as it would help prevent the occurrence.

After my session was complete, I thanked the nurses and we headed out to grab lunch. I spent the afternoon asleep on the couch. I was incredibly tired and didn't realize that I had slept for hours. I woke up with enough time to eat, take the remaining pills scheduled for the day, and head back to bed. I was in bed by 9 pm, which was incredibly early for me. I was on a mission to get well and in order to do so, I needed to listen to my body. If it told me I was tired, I would not fight it and choose to rest instead.

I did not wake up until almost 10 am the next day! I couldn't believe it. That was a record for me.

My morning was spent going through emails and finalizing my October clients for my business. It was very productive. I then had to get ready for an appointment to get injected with a dosage that would stimulate my body to grow more white blood cells. We got halfway to the appointment before noticing that I forgot the vial at home in the fridge, at home. We had to turn back to retrieve the vial before we made our way to my appointment. We got there half an hour late, but we made it. They injected it through my stomach area and sent me on my merry way after discussing some of the side effects.

We made a pit stop on the way home to pick up items for dinner. We made dinner and settled in to watch football for the night. I was still counting down the remaining days for taking pills after this first round. I must mention that taking pills had been the most difficult part thus far.

Day 2 was a total couch potato day. I was impressed that I was able to relax. I napped, watched television, and napped some more. I barely did any projects worth mentioning. I had to psych myself up to take all my medication, but just one more day of pill taking for another 3 weeks. My throat was dry. My taste buds are not functioning properly and my mouth was also dry. I was also finding it very hard to drink water. I was advised to drink lots of water in order to flush the chemo drugs through my system, but it got progressively more difficult to drink it. I was also forbidden from drinking grapefruit juice. My taste buds were already starting to fail me. My food was starting to taste like granulated cardboard.

Life was all about new experiences. I tried on wigs for the first time in my life and I loved them!!! Who would have thought that going through an experience like cancer would have gotten me to step out of my comfort zone like this. It was a family affair. My sister, my mom, and I hit the stores and started shopping. My sister has a gift that was perhaps bestowed upon her for this day, where she could show up for me. Not only does she have an eye for what hairstyle would suit someone, she is also a talented hairstylist in her leisure time. I trust her with all my being with my crowning glory. We accomplished so much in a few hours. I tried wigs and took selfies before narrowing it down to four that I absolutely loved. Of the four, I came home with two. I was definitely going back for two more because they were just too good.

The other new experiences were sore and swollen gums. This was a side effect that I was well aware of, so I was committed to staying on top of maintaining oral hygiene. It was just a matter of time before it happened. I just didn't expect it this soon. I cannot describe the pain. My entire mouth was covered in sores, including close to my throat. Thank goodness I had the mouthwash to ease the pain. Eating was very challenging. Imagine having to eat just for the sake of eating because you cannot taste your food, but it also hurts to eat. There was also the pressure to eat because my chemo dosage was based on my weight, so it needed to be consistent throughout. No one ever said that chemo was easy, but tomorrow is another day.

It had been 4 days since my very first round of chemo. One down, five more to go. There was still that sense of lethargy, but I was starting to feel a bit better. My joints were a bit sore and it felt a bit laborious to walk. It was also my last day with my mother-in-law so we decided to make the best of it by getting an early start by going to the farmers market to gather some goodies for the week. The weather was great and the pickings were even better. The only downside was that I got two tickets on the way to the market. One for speeding and the other for not having my registration documents in the car. Womp Womp! That was an epic fail on my part. It didn't ruin my day though. We had so much more to look forward to.

We went home with all our goodies and decided to make a snack from our finds. Mini farmer's market pizzas were born out of pears, sheep's cheese, tomatoes, onions, walnuts, and spinach.

Next, we headed to my mom's house as she hosted a farewell dinner for my mother-in-law. She had been such an amazing blessing to us. She gifted me with so much of her irretrievable time, to share with me and to ensure that my health was priority, without anyone having to make drastic changes to their daily lives. I felt loved. We laughed, ate, laughed some more, and ate even more before we called it a night. It was time to bid farewell and get to bed.

It was quiet the following day and I just decided to cut my hair off. That wasn't how my day started though. I woke up alone that morning. There was no husband and no mother-in-law. It was an eerie silence. Nevertheless, I spent the day lounging and reflecting. I had these grand ideas of things I wanted to get done, but I was just not up to it. Eventually I got around to checking a few emails and then taking a very long nap. I needed the nap because my entire body from my shoulders down, was in pain. It was unbearable. I was really trying not to rely on any painkillers so the easiest solution for me was to sleep. After a 3-hour nap, I got up with enough time to make dinner and decided that it was time I did something about my hair.

I had no specific plans. I pulled out my braids, wet my hair, and grabbed the scissors. As I cut the first few chunks, I didn't really have anything going through my head. I didn't have any attachment to how it looked once I was finished. I knew that whatever it turned out to be, it was going to be what my hair would look like and I would have to roll with it. I recalled the only time I cut my hair short was about eight years ago, so it would definitely be a change. When I was finished, I looked down at all my hair in a plastic bag, tied it up, washed whatever was left on my head, and marched down the stairs to show my husband my not-so-handy work. He looked and smiled and asked me if I wanted him to use the clippers and make it better. I shrugged and said no worries and off to bed I went. It's as if it wasn't even a big deal. I was, however, very happy at the fact that I could just go to bed feeling a little freer than normal.

I don't know who I thought I was, but I was doing the most. It started with my mom saying she wasn't going to work, instead she was coming over. We decided to hit the mall. My birthday was coming up and I still didn't have an outfit for my dinner party. We strolled around the local mall for a few hours before deciding to grab lunch in the food court and people-watch for about an hour. I couldn't remember the last time I did something like that. Fighting this disease had allowed me to slow down and absorb what was going on around me. It felt great.

We left the mall and headed to my mom's house. I had a birthday party to attend. It was a watch party for the season opener for our Toronto Raptors™ and was guaranteed to be a fun night. My husband, sister, and I made our way to the dinner party. It was everything we needed it to be. Our team was honored at the beginning by receiving their championship rings, they got their championship banner raised and they even won the game. I felt like it was old times. It was probably one of the longest days I have had since surgery, but it was also one of the fun ones.

One week after my first round, and my first bout of nausea set in. It was not severe, but enough for me to throw up just a bit and to start taking the nausea tablets that were prescribed. I was also feeling the pain of having my hair natural. My scalp was incredibly tender and was causing me to have headaches and to feel uncomfortable. Between the nausea, scalp tenderness, and the mouth sores, I felt like I was not winning, but tomorrow is another day.

There were four days remaining until my birthday. In any given year, the month of October would be filled with celebratory plans. If you allow me, I would continue the celebrations into November. This year was totally different. My plans were narrowed down to two things, the annual tradition of the Royal Ontario Museum Friday Night Live party and a birthday dinner. It was the night of the party. We had some first timers on board this year along with some seasoned ROM party goers. Let me set the scene. On Fridays, the natural history museum in Toronto hosts epic parties. Picture roaming the museum but feeling like you were having the time of your life at a club. There were DJs in most of the rooms, as well as food stations and bars. Each Friday night had a theme and this particular one was Halloween. Over 3000 guests would descend on the museum for this affair dressed in some of the best costumes I had ever seen! I must point out that I have never dressed up in a costume for Halloween, but I most certainly enjoyed seeing the creativity of everyone around me.

I have to admit, exploring the museum while drinking and enjoying music had a different feeling. These parties brought together people from very diverse backgrounds all under one roof. There would be guests who were nineteen years old partying with guests who were seventy-five! You would find the white-collar workers with the blue-collar workers all partying and soaking in what the museum had to offer. This party at the natural history museum created a natural ecosystem filled with diversity without much effort. It felt like the natural order of life after all, no man is an island. It was also a good way to wind down the week and a good kickoff to the weekend. This time around, we explored, but I did not partake in alcoholic beverages. It still turned out to be a great way to start my birthday celebrations.

The next planned event was my birthday dinner. I would like to say that it was low-key, but that would be a lie. About thirty of us gathered to have a good time and celebrate. That year had a different type of energy due to my diagnosis. For me, I was grateful to be able to share the moment with everyone. It meant even more to me that year because my family and friends made the time to celebrate with me. I knew they were all praying and sending good vibes and we were all hoping that we could move forward and put this chapter of my life behind us.

So what did I do on my actual birthday? Not much. That was just the way I liked it. Typically, this day is spent doing whatever it is I feel like doing. That birthday was my 40th and it felt different. I woke up for the first time practically bald. The night before, my hair started to fall out as predicted. On one hand, it was fascinating to see how it happened. I was just combing my hair and it started coming out in clumps. I then ran my fingers through my hair and it came out in my hands. I was not married to my hair, as you could tell from the way I chose to cut it short one day. Once the curiosity of it was over, I had my husband break out the clippers and shave it all off. I. FELT. FREE.

Waking up on my 40th birthday feeling lighter due to the lack of hair on my head and feeling free, made for a good start. I lounged in bed and took my time to express my thankfulness for making it to forty years old, especially after being diagnosed with breast cancer. I have always been someone who has been thankful for every day I am blessed with, but this one felt different. I decided I would take a quick drive to Starbucks to get my free birthday beverage and a breakfast sandwich. I started the day being ready to receive. It felt wholesome to give myself the gift of time to fill my cup with love for self and everything around me. There was a sense of internal and external harmony and balance in my new world.

My birthday was now behind me and I was facing round two of chemo. It seemed like time had just flown by between rounds one and two. The process was still the same. The day before treatment, I made my way to the hospital to get blood work done and see the medical oncologist. We discussed how I felt after the previous round and then I was cleared for round two. I returned to the hospital the next day and underwent my second round of chemo. I had become accustomed to the lovely volunteer who would appear mid treatment with a snack cart! He brought me such joy as he doled out cookies and juice. Even though I couldn't really taste much and my appetite was unpredictable, I always accepted whatever he had to offer and saved it for later. I had figured out a way to make my taste buds work for me. There was a window between treatments that would allow me to savor the tastes for a few bites. It was at that time, I would try to enjoy the treats that I cherished. After the usual 2.5 hour stint, I went home and slept like a baby.

With my mother-in-law back home, we had to come up with a new solution for my chemo weeks. Our new regime was that my sisters and mom would be on rotation as my support system during the weeks while my husband went to work while I had scheduled treatments. My baby sister, who is a nurse, would come by on Tuesday evenings so that she, along with my husband, could accompany me to my treatment at the hospital.

She would also be the one to monitor me after treatment and take me in to get my injections the day after chemo. All my chemo appointments were scheduled on Wednesdays, so with each round, the important days were Tuesdays to Sundays. On Thursday evenings, my baby sister tapped out, and my middle sister tapped in. From Thursdays to Saturdays, her job was to drive me anywhere we needed to go, ensure that I was on schedule with my medication, and to keep an eye on my progress. On Saturdays and Sundays, all hands were on deck. My mom would come over with soup on Saturdays and we would hang out all day. On Sundays, they would come over and cook dinner and ensure that I had everything I needed for the week. By Monday, I would begin having a bit more energy. That was my chemo cycle.

With my energy level being as low as it was and no changes in sight until chemo was over, I was trying to set goals and make plans in order to have some sense of normalcy in my life. If I didn't do that, I would lay in bed or on the couch all day. I had no real goals set for the business since canceling our fall events. Aside from our regularly scheduled webinars and blogs, there was nothing that required my immediate attention. We were not due to release our first book until March of the following year. This gave me time to put together a plan. With all the spare time I had on my hands, detailed planning was something I had always dreamt of doing but just never got around to it. I had also started scheduling lunch dates with friends. Everything still tasted like granulated cardboard, but

I tried to schedule lunches the week that I was scheduled for chemo because by then, the medication had started to wear off and I had a slight sense of taste.

I was now at the halfway point of my chemo journey. It was hard to believe time had flown by this quickly. With this third treatment came new side effects. I am thankful to say that I got the mouth sores under control. Also, the state of my head reminded me of an emu—yes, the bird. Over the past month, whatever hair that was left on my head started falling out. My pillow, my washcloth, and any surface that I laid my head on, would result in me seeing trails of little bristles. Now, there was a wisp of hair on the top of my head sparsely spaced—just like the emu I mentioned earlier. The joint pains continued and going for walks was becoming very painful. What new side effects made an appearance? The nail beds of my fingers and my toes started to get a purplish blackish color. My nausea continued. I started packing on the pounds. The list of foods that made me nauseous kept growing. My sense of smell had heightened and there started to be a list of odors that I could not endure. There was a period of a week where I couldn't withstand the smell of the cleaning solution used in our house, even though I have a notorious reputation for hoarding cleaning products. You could find me on any day in the cleaning aisle of any store, checking to see if there was any product I hadn't yet tried. As I looked toward the future in anticipation of what was to come, it seemed like the worst was over.

There was so much to look forward to over the next month. Being at the halfway mark gave me hope. I had a conference to attend and we were planning our annual family getaway. I also planned on making an appearance at the company's annual holiday party. There was one problem. My body was so swollen that I couldn't fit into anything that I owned. After a few days of strolling the mall, I finally found something that would work. The theme of the holiday party was Casino Royale and my outfit, for my sanity, had to have a taste of the theme. All blacked out; black skinny pants, black tank, and a black suede jacket with silver accents, and I was ready to go.

Now that I had my outfit figured out, I shifted my focus to a 2-day event to attend. In between that, I had cultivated the habit of getting massages. My joints had been aching so much, and ever since going for a spa day on my friend's birthday, I had a newfound appreciation for massages.

Can we talk about this event? This was hands down, the best conference I had ever been to. The level of organization that was displayed, the branding of the entire event, the food, the workshops, the people, and all the little intricacies woven into the event. Day 1 of the event brought opening and closing ceremonies that were jam-packed with celebrities. The highlight of the closing session was getting to see Colonel Chris Hatfield—yes, the Canadian astronaut. He gave a moving speech and serenaded us with his beautiful voice. Just when I thought it couldn't get any better, the night ended with an incredible party complete with a live band, culturally themed food stations, an open bar, and stilt walkers!!! If only all business conferences were as well rounded like this.

Admittedly so, I needed to sleep in a bit before tackling day 2 of the conference. After sleeping in, getting my massage and grabbing a coffee, it was time to head downtown to the final day. I managed to make it just in time for a delicious lunch, and spent the afternoon in workshops learning about things I could apply to my business. I also networked and made connections that I was sure to be in touch with going forward.

With the event behind me and a few days to recover, it was now party time! This would be my first time seeing many of my colleagues since my treatment. I must admit it was nice to see them all and to get out to a party. I spent most of my night seated at a table. I am typically the one socializing, dancing, and playing games but this time around, things were different. I didn't have the energy. I stuck around for a few hours before making my exit and left feeling like I was hit by a truck. It was so worth it!

Two days. It took two days for me to recover from going to a holiday party for a few hours. I felt like my body was rebelling. To be honest, I also felt a little angry. I felt like a stranger in my own body. I couldn't wait to get back to the old me. After those two days, I was starting to question if it was worth it to go out for a few hours only to pay a price. It was clear that I would just have to relax and prepare for my next round of chemo.

For the last three rounds, I was on a different drug cocktail than before and was informed about experiencing different side effects. The one positive I looked forward to for those last three rounds was the fact that there were far less pills to be taken each week. I started with my regular Tuesday visit to the hospital for blood work and to meet with the oncologist. I got my green light to proceed as well as additional paperwork regarding the next few rounds and off I went to relax and prepare for what the next day had in store for me.

As the nurse prepared me for the IV, I was relieved to know that the next three rounds wouldn't leave a mark in the injection spot like the previous three did. The change in the cocktail also meant that I wouldn't pee red for the first few days. One thing that was new for this round was that I would have to keep an ice pack on my fingers and on my toes during the treatment. Just imagine me wrapped in a warm blanket with ice packs on all my extremities. Somehow, I managed to sleep through the first 30 minutes of treatment because of the Benadryl IV. After about an hour and a half, it was time to go home. Four rounds down and two more to go. Unlike the first three rounds, I was having a hard time sleeping. I found myself awake until very late at night and in the wee hours of the morning. I had not been taking my regular naps during the day either. My usual post treatment nap just wasn't happening no matter how hard I tried. I decided that instead of fighting it, I would just roll with the punches this time around. Maybe it was one of the side effects of the new drug cocktail. I had been very aware of them especially because now, I had tingling limbs as well as bone pain. I had to shift my focus to the season of decking halls and mistletoes. Instead of tingling limbs, I started to think of jingling bells, instead of bone pains, I began to focus on the most wonderful time of the year.

My husband was leaving to visit his family in the United States for the holiday season and I planned on spending Christmas between my sister's house and my mother's home. We also planned on heading to Blue Mountain for New Year's as this had become an annual family tradition. We had so much to prepare for. I love the holiday season and this was one of the first times in a very long time that I was able to put up the tree early. I finally had the time to focus on fully decorating the house. This was one of the silver linings of this experience. I could never have had this luxury of time before. I blasted my favorite Mariah Carey carols, danced around the house, soaked up the joyous feeling, and thanked the world for this gift. I even spent hours shopping for home decor to add to the spirit of the season. From jolly bathroom towels, holiday scented candles, fuzzy holiday socks, and little knick knacks, I was more than ready for the season. The halls were fully decked, now it was time to celebrate.

The holiday season was out the window as the pain came back in. The pain! I experienced pain like no other. I hurt from the top of my head to the tip of my toes. I could do nothing but curl up in a ball and cry. I cried myself to sleep and then I woke up and cried more. There was nothing anyone could do to help me. I stared at the bottle of Tylenol 3 prescribed to me, but couldn't take one pill. Just the thought of it made me nauseous.

The option was to either throw up multiple times trying to take a pill to make the pain go away or to just hope that it would go away shortly. I spent the entire day in bed and barely ate. All I could do was pray that this level of pain was not going to be typical for each round. I stayed in bed and said to myself that tomorrow is another day.

It was Christmas Eve and I was up at 4 am to drop my husband off at the airport. He was going to spend the holidays with both his mom and his brother in South Carolina. This was a monumental moment for them because it was the first time in many years that they were all spending Christmas together. Normally, one person would not be able to make it due to prior obligations. As I bid him farewell and headed home, I was looking forward to my holiday celebration with my side of the family. I went back to bed and slept for most of the day. I needed to be as rested as possible to enjoy Christmas Day.

It was Christmas morning and our first stop was for brunch at my sister's house. The spread was as expected—glorious!!! She had it all; eggs, bagels, jam, bacon of different varieties, and much more. I tried my best to eat, but I could barely taste the food. Once again, it was like eating dried sandy cardboard. There wasn't enough liquid that would help with the texture or enough spice to enhance the taste. It was so disappointing, but I managed to enjoy the rest of the moment as everyone started opening gifts. It was a great start to the holiday. We left my sister's place and went over to my mother's to start cooking dinner, watching basketball, and hanging out. By the end of the night, I was exhausted. I felt as though I was dragging myself around and needed to rest.

After a few days of relaxing post-Christmas festivities, we left for Blue Mountain. I looked forward to this as we normally didn't consider winter activities for vacation. I had no intention of participating in any winter activities that year, as it was difficult enough to walk. My sister and nephew, on the other hand, were busy snowboarding and skiing while my mother and I watched them go up and down the slopes. We strolled through the village and went in and out of shops and watched the fireworks. After a few days of relaxation and fun, it was time for us to head back to reality. It was a new year and we had new things to look forward to. I, on one hand, was looking forward to finishing cancer treatment and taking a lovely vacation. Together, we were also looking forward to putting this all behind us. My focus was on January 29th. That would be my final chemo treatment, but before that, I needed to get past round five.

My husband returned from vacation and it was time for me to return to my routine of bloodwork, oncology visit, and then chemo. This was the penultimate round and I was growing anxious. I could see the finish line and just needed to make it there. This time around, everything went according to plan and thank goodness there was no intense pain as before. There was pain. My joints seemed to be getting increasingly stiff and my bones were sore, but the pain was not as debilitating as I had previously experienced.

My days were beginning to get longer as the temperature grew colder. I also grew larger. I found myself not wanting to leave the house as I was not a fan of the cold, and I could barely fit into anything I owned. It was beginning to feel depressing. I barely had the energy to move about, so exercising was not something I wanted to do, but I also felt myself growing uncontrollably. I decided that it wasn't worth the stress at that time. I needed to focus on recovery and then I could tackle the weight afterward.

As I approached my final round, I started to wonder about how I would feel once finished. I vowed that I wouldn't cry during that process. I couldn't really help crying in pain, but I could help crying in general. I felt emotional thinking about the sense of relief I would feel at the end of this final round. I knew it wasn't the end of my journey, but it would mark the end of the most difficult portion of my treatment plan. I also started to think of all the things I would be able to do again—like taste my food. I had a few lunch dates that month and although they were a way to motivate me to go out and to meet up with friends, they were a constant reminder of how my taste buds had failed me.

Along with the joy of approaching my final session, there were also other things to celebrate that month. A friend and colleague got married. This was bittersweet as I was scheduled to be at that wedding in Jamaica. Unfortunately, due to my immune system being at risk, it wasn't wise for me to travel. It was a good distraction to be able to sit down with the new bride for dinner before my very last round. I got a play-by-play of their entire time in Jamaica. I felt as if I was there. I was really looking forward to this wedding and if I knew then what I know now, I would've found a way to make it there.

Another bittersweet moment was a lunch date with another friend and colleague. As I was getting ready to wrap up my chemo journey, she was getting ready to start hers. It was such a shock to me when she broke the news about her diagnosis the year before. She was much younger than me and had a toddler to care for. It was such a heartbreaking moment. But being the badasses that we were, we made the best of it. As we sat over lunch, I told her about my experiences thus far. I gave her as much advice as I could and promised to be there for her every step of the way. Her recovery plan was different from mine in that she planned on doing a double mastectomy with reconstructive surgery or getting "stripper boobs" as she called them. Fortunately for her, she was able to plan on recovering eggs for her fertility plan prior to starting chemo. That was a huge relief as she wanted to have more children. It was very difficult to believe that she was in this predicament.

As I walked into the hospital for my final round of treatment, only my husband accompanied me. I had a roller coaster of emotions going through my head. Most of all, I felt light, as if the weight of the world was lifted off my shoulders. During the hour and a half of my treatment, I listened to a podcast to get my mind off what was occurring. As the last drops of the IV went through and the machine started to beep, the nurses started congratulating me on jumping the final hurdle. It was time for me to ring the bell. Ringing the brass bell is a symbol of hope for patients. Here's to hoping I don't ever have to go through this again. I rang the hell out of that bell. I was very relieved, excited, nervous, happy—everything. I had all the emotions. I took some time to thank the nurses and take photos with all the ones who were on shift that day who were involved in my treatment. And with that, chemo was a closed chapter and tomorrow was another day.

7

Radiation

The pandemic was still raging throughout the world and Canada was no different. Can't say it enough how terrified this made me. So when my in person follow up appointment with my medical oncologist was moved to a phone call, I was beyond relieved. This was my first appointment post chemotherapy and radiation. It was great to be able to discuss the next steps, especially when I felt as though I was at the end of my treatment saga. The excitement was palpable. Due to the pandemic, the only downside was that I was not going to be able to celebrate the way I dreamt I would.

As we spoke on the phone, I was able to communicate to my oncologist, how my body was reacting to radiation. It was not without some complications, but in true Dwania form, I did not want to focus on that. I was looking forward, not backward. What was next? What steps did I need to take in order to move toward my new normal? My joints were still very inflamed and the simplest motion was very painful. I yearned to be able to move freely. I wanted to know how long it would take before I could start working out or before the swelling in my entire body subsided. You see, my body felt as if you could poke me with a pin and I would pop. It was also the heaviest I had been in my life. I seriously felt as if I was falling apart.

There was no time for a pity party though. I got reassurance from the oncologist that these were typical side effects for most people. I had to give my body time to heal. I was getting impatient. The weather was starting to warm up outside and I wanted to be able to go for a walk around the block. A one block walk would feel like a marathon to me. My feet were swollen and everything hurt. I still found the space in my mind to be thankful despite all the other feelings I had. There were many people who could not walk so being upset about the notion of not being able to walk a block without discomfort was unreasonable.

We finished up our appointment with the realization that my next step was evident. I had to get started on the hormone treatment component plan. The first part of which was to start taking Tamoxifen as soon as possible. I was also prescribed a monthly injection. With each step of the process, this became a far cry from the first time we met, when I felt information overload. Now I felt like a pro.

While finishing up chemo, I had to reset and start thinking about what it would look like for the business this year. I had to start planning our events. The plan was to slow down, but not to give up altogether. Instead of our regular seminar for the first quarter of the year, we decided to change it up a bit and do something that would require less effort from me in terms of planning.

We decided to host two small scale workshops—one in February and one in March. These workshops would teach entrepreneurs how to create their own signature talks. It was something that I had always wanted to work on for myself as my goal was to speak on large stages especially in a keynote capacity. This workshop was the perfect opportunity to learn how to craft a convincing message that was worthy of being delivered to a crowd. It was intended to be an intimate setting of no more than 10 guests for the first session and no more than 20 for the second. Pulling this off was much easier than doing a full scale seminar which for me, meant less stress. I was trying to make my life as easy as possible.

The planning of these two workshops started with two good samaritans who served as our event venue sponsors. This was a huge relief for me as finding a suitable venue for a reasonable price is always the most difficult step in the planning stage. Now all that remained was to organize catering, swag, workshop host requirements, and advertising. Easy as pie. Typically, I would be concerned about vendors, sponsors, speakers, AV, printing, and much more. I was very thankful that I took the time to put things into perspective and decided to take a different approach to the year.

There is one thing I always look forward to in February and it is Superbowl! My husband's birthday usually falls either on Superbowl or on the weekend of the main event. He is a pretty low key person and doesn't like making his birthday a celebratory spectacle like I do. We decided that we would celebrate by meeting up with some friends at a wing joint to watch the game. I was fresh from my last dose of chemo and I was still having issues with taste and continued to feel pretty lethargic. In order to feel normal, I decided to go out for the festivities anyway. We ate, some of us drank, and we cheered on our teams. The night ended with a win for us and the promise of getting together again sometime soon.

With one celebration behind us, it was time to get some tasks completed before the next celebration in the month. Next stop, back to the hospital. This time it was for my radiation planning session. They simulated a radiation treatment in order to map out the treatment area. I felt like I had a yoga session on my back! I had to hold various positions with very slight adjustments for long periods of time. Once the technicians were satisfied with my position and the location of the beams directed on my body, they proceeded to tattoo me with 5 dots that served as the barriers to the treatment area. The tattooed dots were not noticeable as they looked like small moles. The only difference was that they were dark blue.

Next, I had to go to the radiation wing to get a walk-through of what each visit would look like. The nurse showed me where to check-in each day, where to pick up my gown, and how the scheduling system worked. I was then given my schedule for my first week of radiation and assigned 30 sessions on a Monday to Friday schedule. I was assured that the treatment time would be less than 10 minutes each day for five days per week. I was looking forward to getting started because the sooner it started, the sooner it ended and the faster I healed.

Before we got started, we had a few things to take care of. It was party time!!! My middle sister turned thirty-one that year and we were going out to dinner to celebrate. Unfortunately for me, I had nothing to wear. My body was so swollen that I couldn't fit into anything I owned. It was embarrassing. I went to my trusty store for "whenever I find myself in a bind"—Old Navy. Thank goodness for a sale because I was able to get three dresses for under $60. Getting dressed and looking at myself in the mirror brought me to a new realization—I did not recognize myself. My body was so swollen that my face looked like it was about to explode. I could only equate it to a puffer fish. I was unrecognizable. I began to feel like a different person. There was a level of difficulty to everything I did—even walking was a struggle.

After that shopping experience, despite better judgment, I decided to step on the scale. I almost cried! I was the heaviest I had ever been in my entire life! I had to really put things into perspective in order to not feel completely defeated. It was a tough pill to swallow, but in the grand scheme of things, I was fighting for my life so a few extra pounds wouldn't be the end of the world. I needed to focus on getting past the next treatment step. Once it was behind me, then I could focus on losing the excess weight. Enough of the boohooing! It was time to celebrate.

The dinner party was at a popular Jamaican restaurant in the city. I was salivating at the thought of being able to taste my food. I could not wait to sample some of my favorites. I felt like I would need to retrain my taste buds. I arrived at the restaurant feeling full after a late brunch date with some friends. The plan was to spend the time munching on appetizers and order my dinner to go. It was also a time to see most of my sister's friends who hadn't seen me since my treatment. It was nice to catch up with them and celebrate with my family simultaneously. We ordered practically everything off the menu. I sampled so many things that day and it felt good.

There was one thing left to go before starting radiation. I had to get past my first event of the year. It was an early start to the day and a snowy one at that. There was a snowstorm the previous night and driving to the event venue was going to take at least an hour. I didn't want to do the drive on my own in case I got tired, so I enlisted a friend to carpool. We met up at an ungodly hour of the morning and proceeded to fight our way through the snowy rush hour traffic of the highway. The first 30 minutes of the day was dedicated to ensure that everything was in place for all our guests. We had nine attendees for this workshop. Presentation means a lot to me. I want my guests to have a certain feeling whenever they enter a Canadian Small Business Women's event. They get to feel seen, heard, nurtured, nourished, safe, and welcomed. We laid out swag, hand-crafted name signs, water—both flat and sparkling, and then ensured our catered breakfast was set up and ready for our guests.

Our day was filled with inspiration. A room full of women who were all aspiring to use their voices to share their inspirational stories with the world. As we worked on our signature talks, we started to not only share what stages we would like to grace. We also started sharing stories from our past. It was liberating to be able to feel comfortable enough with a group of people who came in as strangers at the beginning of the day, and left as family by the end. The day wrapped up with our facilitator sharing one of her own signature talks. It shook the entire room. We were even more inspired and felt even more empowered to be vulnerable and to share our stories. That day gave me a chance to reflect on everything I had been through. I had absolute clarity that I wanted to share my story. I hoped that I could be as vulnerable as our facilitator was, to touch, move, inspire, and transform someone else's life.

Radiation started with a meeting with a nurse in the Radiation Department. We started with thoroughly discussing all the things to expect during radiation along with a list of even more side effects to consider. There would be fatigue and there was a very high possibility of skin irritation due to the fact that people with darker pigment have a more severe reaction to the treatment. Relatively speaking, the side effects seemed minimal compared to what I had just been through for chemo. At least this time, I would be able to taste my food and fingers crossed that there wouldn't be any nausea.

With the month "vacation" between chemo ending and radiation beginning, I managed to cram as much as possible into my schedule. In the middle of my radiation prep appointments, I managed to release a book, book a speaking engagement, plan two events, and celebrate Black History Month by attending a few plays. The month of February was productive to say the least. It was strategic on my part as I thought I would have all the energy in the world and I would be motivated by pure adrenaline.

First on the list was a long awaited lunch date with my Girl Gang. We are a group of entrepreneurs turned dear friends who are always there to support each other. We lend helping hands when needed and ears and shoulders too! They have been there for me through some really tough times in both my business and personal life. We dined at one of my favorite hangout spots and caught up on each other's lives. Times like these are priceless. I was starting to feel like I was back on the road to normalcy.

With February being the month, we celebrate Black history and the amazing contribution Black people have made to society; I have always been excited to find ways to support organizations. I am also a big fan of plays and musicals. So when I looked at the list and saw what events were scheduled, it was natural that I had to say yes to some plays. I had the pleasure of seeing Fish & Rum—a play that depicted the relationship between Jamaica and Newfoundland in the 1920s as they traded rum for cod fish. I also saw Caroline for change, starring Canada's own Jully Black. It was a powerful musical dealing with the changes occurring in the deep south of the United States during the Civil Rights era. This musical was also special because my eldest nephew came with us to get his first theater experience. I also got a chance to see a series of plays with another group of close girlfriends. It was a series of short plays by various theater groups in the area. The final musical we had the pleasure of seeing was Hamilton's *You're Welcome*! I had been waiting for a couple of years to get the chance to see it and it did not disappoint me. Experiencing these musicals reminded me of my childhood in Jamaica. My mother was very fond of plays and we went to them often so it was nice to be able to continue this tradition with her.

After spending the weekend recovering, it was time to start the next phase of treatment—radiation. I made my way to the hospital, this time with my mother as my support system. I checked in at the reception desk, changed into the hospital gown, and waited in my treatment area. As they called my name, I was greeted by two wonderful technicians who explained how everything would work. I laid on the "bed" of the machine and they proceeded to adjust both me and the machine until everything was aligned with the tattoos that marked the border of my treatment area. Once aligned, they left the room and the treatment began. It was quicker than I thought. It took about 10 minutes to get everything aligned, but only about 2 minutes for the actual treatment. There was nothing to it. All I had to do was lay there and the machine performed its magic. There was no sensation on my part either. After each treatment, I was told I needed to apply an ointment to the treatment area to minimize the risk of burning or irritation. I decided to always carry a small amount of the ointment and apply it after each treatment prior to changing out of my gown into my street clothes. I wanted this process to be as smooth as possible. All in all, I was only at the hospital for about 30 minutes. If this was what I have to look forward to, I was OK with that!

Five days per week, I would make my way to the hospital for treatment with the same routine. Go to check-in, change into the hospital robe, wait in the unit area in which I was assigned, lay still while the technicians adjusted me, apply the ointment once complete, and then go home. In general, I had no side effects to complain about thus far. I was still lethargic, but nothing compared to how I felt during chemo. The first week of radiation went smoothly. As I finished up on Friday, I was looking forward to doing something I hadn't done in a very long time—take a solo vacation.

I needed a getaway. I really needed some time to clear my head and to really put into perspective everything I just went through. I knew I couldn't go far for this getaway so I settled on Niagara Falls and planned on spending 4 glorious days relaxing. That morning, I packed my suitcase before heading off to my appointment. Once my appointment was complete, I headed back home to load the car and head out for a quick drive. As I made the approximately 1-hour drive to my hotel, I was beginning to feel free and entertained myself during the drive by listening to my favorite podcast—My Favorite Murder. True crime is intriguing to me, especially the back story about serial killers. What was their upbringing like? What made them turn to a life of crime? How do they adapt over time? How do they view themselves? This podcast in particular is unique because it is a true crime comedy podcast. I enjoy the storytelling aspect and the bits of humor inserted throughout. The drive was just enough time to listen to two episodes of the podcast. I got to the hotel, valeted my car, and checked into what would be my home for the next four days. They were kind enough to give me a free room upgrade.

I got to my room and admired the falls that would be my view for the next 4 days. The plan was to do as little as possible when it came to work and to ensure that my feet were up. A late side effect attributed to the chemo was the swelling of my legs. My body itself was swollen and I could feel it in my joints as it hurt to walk or to curl my arms. The swelling of the lower half of my legs was a major concern. Prior to heading to my vacation, I was prescribed water pills as well as compression stockings to try to get the swelling under control. I was ordered to sit as much as possible with my legs elevated and so I rearranged the chairs and table in the room so that I could sit facing the window with my feet propped up. That was my spot.

For 4 days, I only left my hotel room four times—twice to grab coffee from the Starbucks in the lobby and twice to go to the hotel restaurant. My time was spent watching movies, working periodically on creating my keynote talk, napping and staring at the world outside. Uber Eats was on overdrive as all my remaining meals were sourced.

The isolation was a welcomed break for me as it gave me time to reflect on my entire cancer journey. Finding a way to share my experience with others was why working on my signature talk was so important to me. My goal was to use my story to inspire others. Oftentimes we don't look at our experiences as an opportunity for growth. We become down on ourselves. We complain. Some of us are often in the "why me" mode. I understand that not everyone thinks like me. Sharing my thought process throughout this journey as well as my life experiences that groomed my outlook on hurdles I faced, was intended to shift people's perspectives. I worked on curating that talk as well as started to outline where I would like to share my story.

As the days rolled by, I enjoyed watching all the tourists from my hotel window, admiring the falls. The weather was beautiful—not too cold, and very sunny. I yearned to go out for walks and to soak up some fresh air. My swollen legs and sore joints were a hindrance so I had to live vicariously through the little bodies down below as they enjoyed what Mother Nature had to offer. Day by day, I sat in my spot and watched as people walked up and down the parkway. I watched as the water rushed down the falls. I watched the sun set and the night lights dance across the falls. Time passed quickly during those 4 days.

On my final morning, it was bitter sweet. I enjoyed my time on my mini vacation and I didn't want to go back to my regular scheduled life of cancer treatment. There was a bit of anxiety as I drove away from the hotel. Despite my positive outlook in life, I still dreaded having to climb yet another mountain. There were still five weeks of radiation treatment remaining and it couldn't go by quickly enough. I was looking forward to taking a true vacation once it was all done.

There was no point in day dreaming. My focus needed to be on recovery and also finding the joy in the little things. My next adventure was a lunch date with a colleague and friend in another town. Little did I know that this would be my last meal dining inside a restaurant with another human for a considerable amount of time. Let me paint the picture of my "last supper of freedom". It was a relaxing Mexican restaurant. The chef-owner was very well known across the Canadian circuit. As I arrived at the restaurant the smell of seasonings hit me and I could not help but inhale with intention. It smelled good. I couldn't wait to dive in. My friend was already seated and freshly made chips were on the table. We hugged—another thing that I was going to miss dearly—and started admiring the decor in the restaurant. It was not fancy but it was the type of place you would want to hang out. A perfect place for some small bites and a really good beverage that could serve as your local hang out spot. My decision that day was a simple beef quesadilla.

It arrived smelling amazing and I sunk my teeth into it. It was nothing short of delicious. This was the best quesadilla I had ever had—and I have had many. The first few bites were the best for me, especially because food was finally starting to taste good again. This was a rebirth of my taste buds so everything I ate felt like I was tasting it for the very first time. I gratefully savored every bite, all the time remembering when things tasted like granulated cardboard during my chemo treatment.

The conversation flowed and the food was delicious. What more could I have asked for? We wrapped up our lunch date because duty called—my friend had to rush back to work. As I took the 40-minute trip back home, I reminisced on how much fun it was to finally be able to dine with others and enjoy the entire experience. This is what living in the moment was. I had never felt more present than I did then. Each day was a gift and I planned on soaking up every moment. The sun was shining, the weather was great, I just had a wonderful lunch date and I was alive!

As I was still basking in the joy of a great week, we were hit with a once in a lifetime tragedy—a worldwide pandemic. What on earth was that? I was so confused and alarmed and scared. There was news of this Coronavirus going around that was causing death across the globe. People were being affected by this flu-like disease and were winding up in the hospital and dying in record numbers. It had been all over the news and mostly affected Asian and European countries until then. I had been so absorbed in my own life that I didn't really think that it would start affecting us at high rates. Well, here it was.

As my nephew and I headed to my radiation appointment, I started to think of what fun things we could do indoors over the next few days to keep a nine-year-old entertained. Movies, puzzles, art projects, and anything that wouldn't deplete me of all my energy. As we arrived for appointment, the reality of the pandemic was hitting harder. How would we prepare for this? Based on what we had seen on the news, other countries were experiencing shortages in food and supplies. Panic purchasing had set in. I needed to focus on planning, even though I didn't know what I was planning for. As I entered the hospital, I noticed that the check-in process had now lengthened. They were also on high alert and doing everything they could to ensure everyone's safety. It was then that one of the staff informed me that children were not allowed in that particular section of the hospital—for their own safety. Little did I know—remember, I grew up practically living in a hospital as a child. Extreme times called for extreme measures. The hospital staff graciously welcomed my nephew and I as they realized they had to be flexible, given the situation. Not more than 15 minutes later, I was all finished and ready to take on the world. As I greeted my nephew, there was a huge smile on his face along with a handful of candy. Somehow, he managed to win over the team at reception. We thanked them for their hospitality and wished them well as we headed out to stock up on groceries.

I decided to join in on the panic purchasing by pulling into the local Longo's grocery store. It was still very early in the day—10:30 am on a Tuesday morning—but the plaza was bustling with people. While hopping out of the car, I told my nephew to touch nothing. Grabbing a shopping cart and strolling through the aisles of the supermarket was surreal. I saw this stuff on TV, but to experience seeing shelves that were practically bare and seeing essentials in short supply was a reality check. I needed a plan. There were barely any of the essentials—toilet paper, sugar, flour, rice, paper towel, and canned goods. When I saw bags of flour and sugar, I scrambled to grab a few because at that moment, it was about survival. I needed to have food to eat in case we were forced to stay home for an extended period of time. I immediately worried about my other family members. Did they have their essentials? My baby sister, who heard about the State of Emergency, was trying to get a flight out of the reservation where she was stationed for work and I was sure she had an empty fridge. I already didn't like being at the supermarket on a regular day, so panic shopping at that time came with a high level of anxiety. I would just have to do the best I could and make it home in one piece. Those were the moments that made me even more thankful for what I had.

As we reached home and unpacked our bounty, my nephew and I were watching the news to see what was to come. What did a State of Emergency mean anyway? Apparently, we were not necessarily in lockdown like it is in countries like Italy. We were just being ordered to not leave our homes if it wasn't necessary. People who could work from home were encouraged to do so. We were being told not to have contact with anyone outside of our "bubble." There was no certainty about how the virus was contracted and no certainty in how we would prevent it. We were being told to wash our hands regularly because it could also be transferred from surface to surface. All I knew was that my house had become Fort Knox. No one was coming in and hopefully no one would have to go out if it wasn't necessary. The only problem was, my husband was still going into the office.

My nephew and I were taking it day by day. We found a cool 500 piece puzzle to tackle together and planned on watching loads of television. It was still pretty cold outside so we had zero plans on venturing out of the house. This was our time to relax—no school and no work. Little did that kid know that I still had a business to run. With this pandemic making its presence known on Canadian soil, I now had to start thinking of what would be next for us. Our next event wasn't scheduled until May, but we needed to start thinking of plan B immediately.

What a week! It was coming to an end and at least there was some good news in sight. After all the worrying about my sister being able to make it home, she was able to get the last flight leaving the reservation to come back to Toronto. The government had suspended all nonessential travels and airlines were starting to halt passenger aircrafts, so to hear that she was actually on her way was such a relief. Of course my nephew was concerned about his mom during this tough time. He knew he was safe, but he would much rather be with his mother. As she pulled up to the house, the grin on his face was extra wide. Remember that "I got candy" grin from the hospital? It was wider than that. I had secretly already packed all his clothes from earlier in the day. I didn't tell him she was on her way because we wanted to be certain that she made it to Toronto first. Well, she was here! He gave me my hug and ran to the car. I couldn't even allow her to come inside. As I was telling her about the supermarket situation, I was packing as much food as I could spare so that she didn't have to worry about food for the next week or so. All the snacks and the precious flour and sugar were generously divided. With food, clothes, and my nephew in tow, she was off to the comfort of her own home.

We had reached the end of March and the COVID-19 numbers were hyperbolically higher than it was a few weeks ago. Watching the case count climb daily on CNN or listening to what was being reported here in Canada on CP24 was bringing another level of anxiety. The time of my life where I should have been fully focused on being stress free and recovering from what would be one of the most memorable medical experiences I would face, was now being turned into an anxiety driven experience. Death tolls were rising, case counts were rising, and there was no cure in sight. What were we going to do? My daily trips to the hospital were showing ramped up safety protocols. Masks were mandatory. One had to sanitize their hands upon entering. The questionnaire was very thorough and if you didn't have an appointment, you could not enter the building. This was heartbreaking. Imagine having a loved one enter the hospital for treatment or emergency surgery and you not being allowed to see them off. You could not be there to comfort them during their recovery. On one hand, the hospital was not as crowded as it typically was, but on the other hand, it felt eerie. There was no longer that feeling of optimism and safety that I would typically feel when I entered a hospital.

The level of anxiety was palpable, but tomorrow is another day.

8

Rejuvenation

I am not a creature of habit, so having to incorporate something in my life that is expected to occur daily is difficult. I now have the task of having to take a tablet daily for at least the next five years of my life. Taking tablets is already something I don't like doing. I have been this way ever since I was a child. Now, I had to find a way to make it a daily habit. Week one was interesting. I tried to tie in taking the tablet with dinner. So the plan was, before eating dinner, I would take the tablet. I kept the vial in the kitchen on the counter. I was almost certain that I missed a day in the first week. The second week, I had the same tactic, except, I also set a phone timer to go off at 6 pm daily. I was almost certain that I doubled up on one of the nights in the second week. By the third week, I had it down to a science—go figure. I still kept the pill container on the counter and still had the daily reminder on the phone, but I had to find a way to ensure that I did indeed remember to take the dosage. I then started to flip the pill container upside down on the counter whenever I took my pill. So, every night before heading to bed, I would check to see if the container was flipped upside down. If it was, then I did take the pill for the day. I would flip the container right side up every morning before breakfast. This was my new normal.

Along with this new normal, I had to start taking monthly injections to try to put my body into menopause. What an ordeal that was. It was a hefty dose of reality to think that at forty years old, I was being forced into early menopause, but these were the precautions that had to be taken to minimize the risk of the cancer resurfacing. Fortunately for me, I had options when it came to getting the shot administered. Having to battle with healthcare and being in the public during a pandemic was frightening and I appreciated being given the option. I had three options. I could have my sister, who is a nurse, administer the shots, go to the hospital, or go to a local clinic. I chose to have my sister do the deed and use the other options as backups.

The first shot was rather interesting as my sister was not in my "safe bubble" for coronavirus and had not necessarily been in quarantine. I picked up the medication from the pharmacy and forwarded her all the information provided by the hospital. This particular drug came with not only printed directions, but also video tutorials as to how to administer them. Once she was clear on the procedure, it was time for "our" procedure. When she arrived at my house, I had everything in place while she waited in the driveway. I got a pair of gloves and a mask and left them at the door. I had a couple of sheets of paper towel in the bathroom and had the water running. I had the syringe out of the box as well as a sharps container open and ready for use. All she had to do was walk inside, wash her hands for the minimum 2-minute requirement, dry them, dispose of the paper towel, put on her mask and gloves, administer the shot, dispose of the syringe, and gloves in the sharps container, then exit. It went smoothly. We had a no speaking rule in order to minimize the possibility of any germs transferring. Once the shot was complete, she exited. I was then able to speak with her outside from a distance. This was what the pandemic had brought us to. Physical distance socialization.

With all these new habits in my life, I could still look back at all that I had been through and be thankful. There seemed to be a few moments of consistency that had helped to prepare me throughout this entire cancer treatment process. There was the consistency at the beginning of it all with chemo and the medication that had to be taken. There was also the consistency of radiation as that was a 5-day-a-week process that not only involved me going to the hospital consistently, but also required me to be diligent in my self-care process.

Life before cancer was carefree. There was less worry about my health. I felt invincible. Post cancer I had to start looking into myself. I had to listen to my body. I had to begin thinking about what was important, what actually needed to be done, as well as how my actions would impact my body and my health. I also started to look at life very differently. I wanted to live! Live life to the fullest. I didn't want to leave any question of doubt or regret.

I had, and still have incredible doctors on my team. Their treatment plan gave me hope, but I found myself in defense mode. I feared everything. Never in my life did I consider myself to be a pessimist and a negative person, but I thought of the negative outcome to all actions in my life. While going for a walk, I would imagine that the person on the other side of the street would attack me, or that the person driving their car would lose control and run me over, or a dog's leash would come loose and I would be mauled. This was a daily occurrence. It became exhausting and very anxiety heavy. It was time to get a therapist involved.

The suggestion to get a therapist came from my oncologist and I could not have been more thankful. He stressed the importance of putting in the work on my end to recognize what I have been through as well as to work on healing the mental and emotional components. I didn't know the first thing about finding a therapist, but I decided the best thing to do was to ask for referrals and do my research. I didn't have many requirements except that I really wanted to find someone who was of the same background as myself so that they would be able to understand my cultural references as well as how I grew up. We had our first virtual meeting to "get to know each other" before I made my final decision.

If you have never ventured into the world of therapy, I implore you to give it a try. In the Black community, historically, we were advised to pray about it or told that we are strong. We have been suppressing or dismissing traumatic life experiences instead of curing them. My therapy sessions were exactly what I needed. They were eye opening and allowed me to tap into the reasons why I had an irrational fear of life. I learned exercises to implement daily to counter all the fear and negativity that governed my life. I had diagrams to guide me through my feelings. Therapy came at the perfect time. As soon as I started to get the hang of things, it was time to make another emotional decision.

It was coming up on the two-year mark since I started chemo. In the space of two years, I started and finished chemo, started and finished radiation, celebrated two birthdays, addressed my mental health, started a workout regime, found ways to safely enjoy the summer sun, and jumped right back into work mode. With all that behind me, my next hurdle happened to be another surgery. I had to make the difficult decision to remove my ovaries and my fallopian tubes. It was not a decision I took lightly. As I sat in my oncologist's office and he made the recommendation, the thought of another surgery brought tears to my eyes. I had a choice to make. Either I agreed to move forward with the surgery to decrease the chance of cancer returning or not. My mind was once again, going in circles. My oncologist answered all my questions and laid out the process. As I made the final decision to move forward, it was as if I held my breath for the entire appointment. I had to be sure that it was what I wanted to do. Walking to the car, I was in a daze. I wasn't questioning my decision, but instead there was a feeling of conclusiveness.

As I got to the car, I felt the tears in my eyes. I sat in the parking lot and rationalized my feelings. As a woman, this felt like cancer was taking away my woman-hood. I had no children and the finality of it boiled to the surface. Using some of the exercises I learned in therapy helped me to move past that moment and start the short trip home to prepare for the next step. I had a new doctor to meet!

As I walked into a new medical space, this time surrounded by pregnant ladies, my reality came to the forefront again. Meeting with the surgeon was very reassuring. I was going to undergo a surgery that was a common procedure and thankfully laparoscopically—which meant that the healing process would not be as intensive as if I would have had to have a cut right across the bottom of my stomach area. The surgery date was set for four days before my birthday.

Surgery during COVID-19 was a new experience. On the morning of, I was dropped off at the door of the hospital because no one was allowed in with me. I went through the check-in process alone and made my way to the surgical area. As I was briefed about the surgery, I found joy in the solace of a quieter hospital. Once again, I sashayed down the runway of the surgical hall right into my surgical room, greeted my medical super heroes, and laid on the bed awaiting the entry into my anesthetized nap. I looked to my right and thanked everyone in advance for their work, then looked to my left, to find my surgeon huddled in a circle with her team, praying and hitting play on her playlist. This felt like a true Grey's Anatomy moment.

I woke up a few hours later feeling bloated and groggy, but thankful that another hurdle was behind me in the race of my life. I got dressed and a lovely volunteer wheeled me out to the front of the hospital to my waiting family, and off I was to rest at home. The following few days were met with exhaustion and discomfort. It was almost my birthday and all I could feel was sadness and pain. I had to start digging deep to find the joyful moments as this year; the celebration was much smaller than I would have liked. A party of three was what was on the table. It was much different from the vibe from a couple of years previously, but it would have to do. As disappointed as I was by the circumstance, I was thankful to be alive to experience it. There were too many people who didn't get to celebrate moments like those.

My mind was set on moving forward. The focus was on healing physically and mentally. Not only did I beat cancer, I planned on beating this pandemic as well. There was still a level of fear of getting sick, but I vowed to not allow it to stop me from making my way toward feeling free again. I had many tomorrows to experience.

CONCLUSION

Freedom!

COVID-19 and cancer are now behind me. The past few years have been a lesson in living life to its fullest. The experience has been life-changing, but I will not allow it to define me. Looking back, I cannot wrap my head around everything I went through. Now that I have a clear head and am technically no longer in the thick of it, I feel a high level of sympathy for the old me. I didn't exactly FEEL at the moment. I was too busy worrying about everyone else other than reacting on my true feelings. I truly appreciate the journey I went through and am thankful that therapy was a part of my recovery process because it taught me how to embrace my feelings.

The new me doesn't come free of challenges. I have learned to accept everything about myself as it is, not as I would like it to be. The first thing on the list is my body. It is very new to me. There are daily aches and pains. My body shape is drastically different. I have the choice of either stressing about losing weight or living my life in the present. I choose the latter every single day. The new me also comes with a ball of emotions that I am not afraid to express. If I am sad and I want to cry, I will cry. If something makes me uncomfortable and does not bring me joy, then I no longer want to be a part of it. My plan is to enjoy this life.

My new era of freedom involves me spending more time with family and seeing the world. I have to make up for all the low key birthdays of the past few years because celebrating another year of life means more now than ever. Birthday celebrations have always been a huge deal in my life and I want to get back to that. I remember the first huge "birthnight" celebration I had when I was eight years old. If you are not Jamaican, allow me to explain the concept of a "birthnight" party. It's a celebration that involves the entire family, your friends, and their families as well. As the name suggests, it's a party that occurs at night. The menu is not your average burgers and hotdogs. It is the menu of the island. Think rice and peas, jerk chicken, jerk pork, roast fish, curried goat, and a soup of some sort. There are dominoes and card games and music and all the fun party festivities you can imagine and of course—cake! The children and the adults would eat and dance the night away. Those memories are ones that I will always cherish.

Cheers to making more memories and celebrating each day as if it's your birthday.

Remember, tomorrow is another day.
One love!

Book Club Questions

1. *How did the author's personal journey through cancer treatment impact your perspective on resilience and overcoming challenges?*

---

2. *The author describes the medical profession as superheroes who saved her. How did this portrayal influence your perception of healthcare professionals and their role in patient care?*

---

3. *Throughout the book, the author shares moments of laughter, tears, and raw emotions. Which scenes or anecdotes resonated with you the most, and why?*

---

4. *In what ways did the author's storytelling style enhance your understanding of the lesser-known aspects of cancer treatment? Were there any surprises or revelations for you?*

---

5. ***"Tomorrow Is Another Day" is described as a love-letter to life and the island that made the author. How did the setting and cultural background contribute to the narrative and themes of the book?***

---

6. ***The author emphasizes that this is not a story of sadness, but one of resilience and realization. How did this perspective shape your reading experience, and what message did you take away from it?***

---

7. ***Reflecting on the book, how has it influenced your own outlook on life, adversity, and the importance of cherishing each moment?***

---

8. ***What lessons or insights did you gain from the author's journey that you can apply to your own life, whether facing challenges or embracing the joys of everyday living?***

---

9. ***The author invites readers to join her on this journey. How did you personally connect with the author's experiences, and what aspects of her story do you think will stay with you long after reading the book?***

---

10. ***If you could ask the author one question about her experience or the writing process of "Tomorrow Is Another Day," what would it be?***

To book Dwania McLarty-Peele as a speaker at your book club meeting or your event, email her at:
bookings@canadiansmallbusinesswomen.ca

ACKNOWLEDGMENT

This book has been a labor of love. It started out as a journal of my daily experiences once I started my cancer treatment and turned into something so cathartic that I wanted to share it with the world.

Thank you to the team at Credit Valley Hospital. Your dedication knows no bounds.

Thank you to my family and friends for all your love and support. I know it was a difficult time for you, but you came together to ensure that I was in a good place. Thank you to my mother, Susan, for all those trips back and forth with me to the hospital, my Saturday soup deliveries and your daily check-ins to make sure I was resting and eating well. Thank you to my sisters, Ginel and Doujoné for keeping me entertained and reminding me that life still exists even when you are battling something as grand as cancer. Thank you to my nephews Darius and Jacob for giving me the gift of pure joy through the eyes of children. Sometimes, I needed the reminder of what a care-free, responsibility-free life of joy looks like. Thank you to my loving husband for being my support system through the physical and emotional turmoil throughout this entire process.

Thank you to my mother-in-law, Bonita, for dedicating her time to ease some of the pressure during this time.

My friends! Too many of you to list. You know who you are. No one has better friends than I do.

Thank you, Shirin, for helping me paint a clearer picture with words.

Thank you, Ambika, for being my sanity check and for lending your time to read the manuscript and give me that "real talk" critique before submission. Thank you also for reminding me of what a badass I am!

Thank you to my community—Canadian Small Business Women—for understanding when I took some time off to write instead of making myself available for events and strategy sessions.

Most of all, thank you, dear reader, for purchasing this book. My hope is that you are encouraged to live your life fully and to also serve as a reminder to make that doctor's appointment!

About the Author

Dwania McLarty-Peele is the Founder of Canadian Small Business Women, a company that supports aspiring and current female entrepreneurs. She is a forever optimist and her favorite mode of relaxation is sipping a cocktail and soaking up the sun—after all, she is a Jamaican girl. She currently lives in the outskirts of Toronto, Canada. She is a graduate of St. Clair College and The University of Windsor. Some of her other publications are *The Power Within: Inspiring Stories of Female Immigrant Entrepreneurs* and *Voices of Strength: Inspiring Stories of Female Entrepreneurs.*

Contact with author at:

@dmpeele

@CdnSmallBizWmn

@canadiansmallbusinesswomen

@canadiansmallbusinesswomen

canadiansmallbusinesswomen.ca

Gratitude Planner

Grab your FREE 7-Day Gratitude Planner

Attention, dear readers!

As a token of gratitude for your support and engagement, we're excited to offer you a FREE 7-Day Gratitude Planner inspired by the themes of resilience and positivity found in "Tomorrow Is Another Day." This planner is designed to help you cultivate a mindset of gratitude and resilience as you navigate life's challenges.

Join Our Group

Join our "Tomorrow Is Another Day" Facebook group!

Chat with the author.

Share personal stories.

Celebrate resilience.

Share your thoughts on the book.

Made in the USA
Columbia, SC
27 April 2024

34970162R00098